THE ECCLESIOLOGY OF WATCHMAN NEE & WITNESS LEE

THE ECCLESIOLOGY OF WATCHMAN NEE & WITNESS LEE

BY JAMES MO-OI CHEUNG

CHRISTIAN LITERATURE CRUSADE
Fort Washington, Pennsylvania 19034

CHRISTIAN LITERATURE CRUSADE
Fort Washington, Pennsylvania 19034

CANADA
1440 Mackay Street, Montreal, Quebec

GREAT BRITAIN
The Dean, Alresford, Hampshire

AUSTRALIA
P.O. Box 91, Pennant Hills, N.S.W. 2120

SBN 87508-088-X

Quotations from:

Scripture, from the *King James Version of the Bible* unless otherwise indicated.

The Living New Testament, © 1967 by Tyndale House Foundation. Used by permission.

The New American Standard Bible–New Testament, © 1960, 1962, 1963 by The Lockman Foundation. Used by permission.

What Shall This Man Do? by Watchman Nee. © Angus I. Kinnear. Victory Press and Christian Literature Crusade. Used by permission.

The Normal Christian Church Life by Watchman Nee. Revised edition © 1962 by Karl Hammond. International Students Press. Used by permission.

My Uncle, Watchman Nee by Stephen C. T. Chan. The China Alliance Press. Used by permission.

The Greek New Testament by Henry Alford. Copyright © 1958. Moody Press, Moody Bible Institute of Chicago. Used by permission.

Protestant Biblical Interpretation by Bernard Ramm. Baker Book House. Used by permission.

A Historical Sketch of the Brethren Movement by H. A. Ironside. Zondervan Publishing House. Used by permission.

A Manual of Ecclesiology by H. E. Dana. Central Seminary Press. Used by permission of Southwestern Baptist Seminary.

Material from Chinese sources has been reproduced in the author's own paraphrase. This includes English titles of Chinese works.

To

My Parents

CONTENTS

INTRODUCTION

The inspirational writings of Watchman Nee on the subjects of salvation and sanctification have been translated into many languages and read by thousands of believers all over the world. Many lives have been changed and many wearied spirits uplifted by his message. In recent years Nee's teachings on the doctrine of the church have also become very popular. However, unlike his writings on the nature of the Christian life, which have obtained universal acclaim, his ecclesiology has become very controversial, partly because of its relentless denunciation of denominationalism and partly because of the new emphasis it has received when put into practice by Witness Lee and his followers.

In order to understand fully and evaluate fairly the controversial subject of the ecclesiology of the "Little Flock,"[1] we need to take into consideration all aspects of their thought and weave them together to furnish a total picture. This book is an attempt to meet this need and to help those interested in the "Little Flock" movement to make their own evaluation with a fuller understanding.

I am not unaware of the discrepancies that often exist between ideal and practice. "Little Flock" critics have pointed out that the "Little Flock" adherents fall far short of what they write and advocate. How much of this is true cannot be fairly determined now because, as their

---

[1]They used no name to designate themselves; this name was used by outsiders and was taken from *The Little Flock Hymnal* which they published. We use the name here only for the sake of convenience.

contemporaries, we lack historical perspective. It is far more important that we evaluate the ideas of the men and not their doings at this juncture. On the other hand, the unorthodox teachings and practices that Witness Lee (the present "Little Flock" leader after the imprisonment of Watchman Nee) and his followers are accused of in recent years call for some remarks. The two articles written by Rev. Elisha Wu, which I have translated and put in the appendix, should provide the reader with a glimpse of the recent development in ideas and practice in the "Little Flock" circle. Rev. Wu is a famous Chinese writer and journalist, well known for his staunch defense of the truth of God. He is presently pastor of Winnipeg Chinese Alliance Church in Manitoba, Canada.

As founder, prophet, and leader of the movement, Nee provides us with almost all the distinctive features and basic teachings of the "Little Flock" ecclesiology. However, there are still some important things in the field of ecclesiology that we cannot find in Nee's writings. In order to give a comprehensive view of the "Little Flock" thinking on the church we have to go also to the writings of Witness Lee, the other exponent and spokesman of the "Little Flock." A close associate of Nee, Lee worked for a good number of years with Nee in Mainland China. It is natural, therefore, that he embraces the basic teachings of Nee with little deviation. However, it should not be assumed that Nee would agree to all that Lee has to say in the area of ecclesiology, especially when we remember that in recent years many, both inside and outside the "Little Flock," have accused Lee of teaching heresy in some other matters. Foes of Witness Lee should be reminded, however, that not all that Lee teaches is heresy. In light of the controversy over the figure of Witness Lee I have been very careful in specifying throughout the book the sources of different ideas, whether they are from Nee or from Lee.

The first chapter deals with the life and ministry of

Watchman Nee, who started the movement. I am thankful to Rev. Stephen Chan, editor of the famous Chinese *Bible Magazine,* for his permission to use the series of articles he wrote on his uncle Watchman Nee. The articles have subsequently been published in book form as *My Uncle Watchman Nee.*

The second, third, and fourth chapters deal with the "Little Flock" ecclesiology proper. No analytical comments are made in the text of these chapters even though I may not agree with some of the ideas presented. This gives the reader an opportunity to form his own opinions as he reads along.

On the other hand, any independent and objective study of a certain system of thought in the controversial field of ecclesiology would be incomplete if no evaluation and criticism were advanced. Thus in the last chapter I attempt to examine the key thoughts of the "Little Flock" ecclesiology and make some critical comments. These are offered not as the last words on the subject in question, but as points of reference from which the reader may form his own conclusions. They are also intended to stimulate thinking and further discussion.

Chinese names have been rendered according to the romanization used in *Matthew's Chinese-English Dictionary.*

The greater part of this book was originally written as a thesis for my Master of Arts degree at Trinity Evangelical Divinity School. A special word of gratitude is due Dr. Robert Culver, under whose encouragement the topic was initially chosen. His guidance and that of Professor Herbert Kane in the course of the project is deeply appreciated. I also want to extend my sincere appreciation to Mr. Barnabas Liu and Mr. Peter Chang for their generous gifts of many volumes of Watchman Nee books.

I would also like to thank the following publishers for allowing me to quote from their books: The Christian Literature Crusade of Fort Washington, Pennsylvania; the Central Seminary Press of Kansas City, Kansas; the

International Students Press of Washington, D.C.; The Lockman Foundation, of La Habra, California; Baker Book House, Grand Rapids, Michigan; Zondervan Publishing House, Grand Rapids, Michigan; Moody Press, Chicago; and The Alliance Press, Kowloon, Hong Kong.

A very special word of appreciation is also due Dorothy, my wife, whose remarkable labors at the typewriter make me all the more thankful to the Lord for giving me such a wonderful helpmate and co-laborer in His service.

Fort Worth, Texas   James Cheung

Chapter 1

WATCHMAN NEE AND HIS MOVEMENT

Watchman Nee is a native of Fuchow, the capital city of Fukien Province. His grandfather was the first Methodist pastor in China, known to be a zealous and devoted preacher. A requirement of ancient tradition was that he marry a girl of the same province. However, when he could not find a suitable Christian girl in Fuchow, he gladly chose a fine Cantonese Christian girl to be his life partner, thus putting his faith before custom and tradition.

Nee's father, Nee Wen Hsiu (倪文修), grew up in a Christian home and received a fine Christian education. Later he moved to Swatow, Kwangtung Province, to work for the Fukien customs office. He was known to be an amiable and good-natured gentleman, quite unlike his wife who was always harsh and severe. Born in 1877, Nee's father lived for sixty-three years and died in 1940.

Nee's mother, Lin Ho Ping (林和平), also came from a Christian family. The first child she bore her husband was a daughter, and so was the second. This greatly frustrated her, living as she was in a feudalistic Chinese society which prized the male above the female. The gossip and scornful remarks of relatives drove her to her knees, though at that time she was only a nominal Christian. She prayed earnestly: "O God, if you give me a son, I'll give him back to you and let him serve you all his life." Her prayer was answered quickly. The next year, 1903, Watchman Nee was born. He was first named Shu Tsu (述祖).

During his boyhood days Nee Shu Tsu was a very active and mischievous youngster who was constantly ruining furniture or knocking over vases. This brought him many beatings from his strict and severe mother. When playing with either brothers and sisters or neighboring children, Shu Tsu always took a leading part and initiated all kinds of new tricks. From his very early days he fully displayed his gift of leadership.

Later, when the family moved back to Fuchow, Nee's father hired a private tutor to teach his nine children the traditional Four Books and Five Classics. Young Nee Shu Tsu proved himself to be an excellent student of very high caliber, scoring the top grade most of the time. Having grounded himself in the Chinese classical studies, he was sent to the Trinity Middle School (三一中學), conducted by the Anglican Church. There also Shu Tsu always received the highest honors in class.

In the year 1922, when Shu Tsu was nineteen, Miss Dora Yu (余慈度) came to Fuchow to conduct a series of revival meetings. Nee's mother attended and was interested in the message. One day about this time a decorative piece was found broken at home. Nee's mother, without a careful investigation, decided that it must have been broken by Shu Tsu, the naughtiest of the nine brothers and sisters, and gave him a very severe beating. But Shu Tsu was innocent this time; so in his young heart he bore a grudge against his mother. When his mother later asked him to attend Miss Yu's meetings, he refused. However, in one of these meetings Mrs. Nee became a born-again Christian, and began to deal with her sins. Immediately she thought of her mistreatment of her son. She went to him and asked him for forgiveness. This was a very strange thing to do in a Chinese society. It touched the tender heart of Nee Shu Tsu, and out of curiosity he went to hear Miss Yu, who thus became instrumental in his conversion.

The first thing Nee did after his conversion was to deal with his sins. At school Nee was doing well in all subjects except the course in Bible knowledge, in which he always failed to score a passing mark. This had greatly hurt his pride, and so he had stooped to cheating. What he did was to write the important verses on his palms. The long sleeves which were in fashion in those days concealed his palms, so the practice was not detected. This cheating had brought him a passing grade. Now, under the convicting power of the Holy Spirit, he was moved to confess this sin. For a conceited student like Nee, who always won the highest honors in class, this was not an easy thing to do. Moreover, the consequence of such an offense was always expulsion from school. For Shu Tsu this also would mean the loss of an opportunity to be sent to a well-known university in the country after graduation. However, such considerations did not prevent him from making his confession to the principal of the school. God honored the great price that Nee paid, and he was not expelled.

Sometime after his conversion he began using the name To Shen (柝聲), which is roughly translated "Watchman." *To* is the bamboo drum or gong used by the town watchman on his night rounds, and *shen* is the sound it makes. It is not known why he chose this particular name, or if it was given him by someone else.

After his conversion Nee met two missionaries through Miss Yu: Miss M. E. Barber and Miss L. S. Ballerd. These two women, who worked together in Fuchow from 1920 on, had a very great influence in shaping the spiritual life of Watchman Nee. Both missionaries had the same conviction, that the spiritual condition of China depended on the spiritual awakening of her young people. After praying for almost ten years, first separately and then together, their prayers were answered by the revival that broke out in Fuchow under the leadership of Miss Yu in 1922. In those meetings God raised up a group of young men who later became devoted servants of God in preaching the gospel in all parts of China. Among them, besides Watchman Nee, were Wang Tsai (王載　　), Wang Lien Chün (王連俊　), Wang Tse (王峙　), Miu Shao Hsün (繆紹訓　), and Luke Chung Hsin (陸忠信　). The life and thinking of Nee were further influenced at this time by the writings of Mrs. Jessie Penn-Lewis and Mr. D. M. Panton of England.

The woman who became Nee's wife, Chang P'in Hui (張品蕙.), was a childhood friend of his, their two families being close friends. But at the time when Nee was converted and dedicated his life to the Lord's work, Miss Chang was still a non-believer. After much prayer and consideration, Watchman Nee decided that such a worldly and vain girl could not serve the Lord with him. Thus the two parted. Yet ten years later they met again in Shanghai. By that time, however, she had accepted the Lord, and also had been graduated from the famous Yen Ching (燕京　) University. They were married when Nee was about thirty. Mrs. Nee, with her training in literature, later became a great help to Nee in his literary endeavors.

Watchman Nee began his preaching ministry at about the age of twenty. At that time he was still attending Trinity Middle School, which would give him, upon graduation, the equivalent of two years of university. He started by conducting meetings with a few friends. They wore gospel jackets and used gospel pictures, simple hymns, and a big gong. Later they rented a small house for their work. This lasted until 1927, when the original workers separated because of differences of opinion and in vision.

This year marked a turning point in Nee's ministry, for after 1927 Nee moved his headquarters to Shanghai. The work in Fuchow was left in the hands of Wang Lien Chün, and then Chang Ch'i Chên (張 敏 珍), until the Communists took over the country in 1949. His unusual concept of the church and the different way of founding churches brought Nee many friends and many enemies. From this time on Nee's new movement began to spread widely, and the number of churches grew rapidly in China. From 1923 to 1950 Nee founded two hundred churches under the principle of "one church at one locality."

The way Nee founded churches in China was very simple. He always began with a small group of people meeting in a house. When the people became spiritually mature and the number grew, then they began to think about a church building. The first "local church" was established in Fuchow in the year 1923, with no special name given to the church. In the same year he also founded the magazine *The Present Testimony* (復 興 報).

The first name Nee gave to his church was "A meeting in the name of the Lord in X X (name of place)." Later he changed it to "the Christian meeting place" (基 督 徒 聚 會 處). After 1948 it was called "the Church of God." But because this was a name used by some other churches he finally changed it to "X X (name of place) Church." The titles "assembly" and "meeting" were abandoned. Outsiders called them "The Little Flock," a name they got from their hymnal called *The Little Flock Hymnal.* The name "Little Flock" is, of course, taken from Luke 12:32.

These two hundred churches founded by Nee were very strong spiritually, and not only self-supporting but also very wealthy. This formed a striking contrast to the financial dependence and spiritual stagnation of the other churches, which were denominational in character. The secret of Nee's success lay in his emphasis on the deepening of the believers' spiritual life through intensive training in the Word of God. While the responsibility for expanding the work of the church lay chiefly, if not solely, on the shoulders of the pastor in the denominational churches, Nee concentrated on training all the believers to do the work of God. Nee also saw very clearly that the measure of the progress of a church was not only in the expansion of the work of the church, but also in the growth and maturing of the spiritual life, both individually and corporately. Nee truly fed his flock. From the content of *The Present Testimony* published by Nee, it can be discerned that he made the deepening of the believers' spiritual life the special ministry of the journal. From 1928 to 1930 the theme of the magazine was: "A special discourse on the Lord Jesus Christ, with special emphasis on His life, death, resurrection, intercessory ministry, bodily return, and His future Kingdom." The purpose of the magazine was stated as "The fostering and cultivation of the spiritual life, with no attempt to debate rationally." From 1931 on there was no mention of the purpose of the magazine. The theme was rephrased to read: "A special discourse on the profound things of God." From 1932 to 1934 the magazine had for its theme: "A special discourse on the principles of the spiritual life." By the year 1932 Nee received many complaints from readers about the profound and specialized nature of the magazine, and requests to make the message simpler in form so that more people could understand. Nee replied to his readers by saying that the magazine was published not for all Christians, but only for those who were truly seeking to deepen their spiritual life. The magazine was for those who had spiritual needs, and not for those without spiritual needs. Nee had the conviction that he must not come down to the low spiritual standards of the majority of shallow Christians. Instead he expected such Christians to measure up to his standards. If because his congregation has not become very advanced in spiritual things a preacher merely cracks a few jokes and tells a few stories in his sermons, God's people will never grow. Watchman Nee has surely proved that we cannot concern ourselves merely with making new converts and omit giving them intensive training in the Word of God and the deepening of their spiritual lives after they have come to Christ. Evangelism and training must go hand in hand, or the church will forever be full of spiritual infants who hinder the progress of the church.

The book *Rethinking Our Missions*[1], published in 1938, represents Nee's thinking on church matters. This is a book compiled from lecture notes taken from his talks to his co-workers. An abridged version of this book was published earlier under the title *The Life of an Assembly* (聚會的生活). Another book by Nee that deals with the church is *The Orthodox Tradition of the Church* (教會的正統). In these writings Nee considers denominationalism as a sin. It is denounced in Galatians 5:20 ("seditions, heresies [factions—NASV]") as a sin of the flesh. Believers must not only seek to pull out of such "condemned organizations" themselves, but should also try to lead others out of such establishments. He also asserts that churches must be established accord-

[1]The title in English is *The Normal Christian Church Life*. The English version is an abridgement of the Chinese original.

ing to locality as in the New Testament. There should be only one church in one locality. All these local churches must have administrative and financial independence. Nee thus insists that we must stand on a non-denominational ground to build up the church according to the pattern set forth in the New Testament.

Watchman Nee's preaching and practice of the doctrine of the local church made a tremendous impact on the churches in China. They were all forced to react to his ideas one way or another, favorably or unfavorably. There were many who were convinced by his ideas and left their own denominations to join him. There were also others who came to see the same light, yet who could not agree with all the practices of the "Little Flock"; so they started their own non-denominational churches. Then there were the leaders of denominational churches, who were naturally much offended because of the members who left their denominations as the result of the influence of Nee. They first attacked Nee for stealing their "sheep." Soon they came to the realization that this would not do. They must find out why their people had left their own churches to join Nee. This stimulated them to seek deeper into Biblical truth concerning the church. They also found out that they did not provide as well for the spiritual edification of the people of God as the "Little Flock" did. Another important influence that Nee's movement exerted on the various denominational churches, which had thus far been supported by mission funds, was to make them see the fact that they should no longer depend on foreign churches to support them. If the "Little Flock" could be self-supporting, they too could educate and encourage their own people to give.

Besides making a contribution to the understanding

of the concept of the church, Nee has also given to the church in China a clearer concept of the doctrine of salvation. Many think of the gospel as a piece of good news just for the unsaved. But in Nee's preaching the believer needs the gospel of salvation as much as the non-believer. The cross is not only effective for the sins of the past, it can also save us from the sins of the present. A dominant theme in Nee's preaching is the possibility of living a victorious life because of the negative work of the cross operating on our sinful nature and through the positive work of the life of Christ in us. "We live an exchanged life and not a changed life," declares Nee. According to him, it is no use for us to strive to do good. Let Christ do it in us. It is not we but Christ who lives in us. We find such themes repeated again and again in his books, such as *The Spiritual Man, The Normal Christian Life, Sit, Walk, Stand,* and *The Release of the Spirit.*

Besides church planting and preaching, Watchman Nee was also very successful in his literature ministry.

It was when he was about twenty, when he first stepped out to do the Lord's work, that he founded the magazine *The Present Testimony,* as mentioned before. Nee did not intend his magazine to treat a variety of topics catering to all kinds of Christians. It was published for those who were seeking spiritual maturity. It endeavored to present to the people of God the message God intended for the time—to experience the work of the cross of His Son, so as to build up the Body of Christ fit for the coming of God's Kingdom. Besides *The Present Testimony* Nee was also responsible for putting out two other publications: *The Christian Post* (基督徒報) and *Sermon Records* (講經記錄). All these magazines contain the sermons of Nee. Other than those appearing in the early issues of the magazines, however, most of the articles were not actually written by Nee himself, but were sermons he had preached which others had recorded. Many of these articles were also published in book form later. *The Present Testimony* was originally intended to be a monthly periodical. However, because of financial shortage it came out whenever enough funds were received, sometimes every four months and sometimes every two months.

The most important book, and the only one that was actually written by Nee himself, was *The Spiritual Man*. It is a three-volume work of over one thousand pages and four hundred and fifty thousand words (in Chinese). The entire work was completed on the 25th of June, 1929. After that he fell sick for a long period of time. From 1926 to 1932 he was in poor health most of the time.

Nee also edited *The Little Flock Hymnal*. He started this project at the end of 1927. The first volume contains 127 hymns. Nee wrote some of them, but most of the others were translated from English. One or two were written by Miss Ting Su Hsin (丁素心教士).

Another characteristic of Nee's ministry was his total dependence on God for his supplies. Once he was invited to go to a certain place five hundred miles away from Fuchow. At that time he had only a little over thirty dollars, which was only one-third of the fare. The day before he started on his journey he was moved by the Holy Spirit to give twenty dollars to a friend of his. After some hesitation and much prayer he took the money to his friend. Next day, when he arrived at the first stop he had only ten dollars left, which was not enough to get him to his destination. While he was wondering whether he should go back to Fuchow he asked himself why did he not pray to God for a cheaper fare to get to his destination. After he had prayed, the operator of a motor launch came to ask if he was going to Chien Yin—the very place he was wanting to go. He offered to take him there for only seven dollars. On the boat he inquired about the reason for the cheap fare, and found out that it was a government boat which accommodated only one passenger, and that at a low rate. After the meetings Nee had no money to go back. Although at the farewell dinner a believer had asked if he could pay for his return passage, Nee had not liked the way he had offered him the money and had refused. On his way to the pier he prayed earnestly for the needed fare. Before long the person who had offered him the fare before came back and insisted that he must let him have a share in the work. This time Nee accepted the money and returned home.

Nee never accepted other people's money indiscriminately. Once a relative of his sent him two hundred dollars. When he received the money he had a little misgiving because his relative was only a nominal Christian. He decided to write back and find out whether his relative was giving him the money as a Christian or as a relative. When he got the reply that the money was given as a relative, he accepted it.

A thrilling story of faith was told by Nee himself. Once he went with a few brothers to an island to conduct some evangelistic meetings. All the inhabitants of the island were idol worshipers. One day one of his co-workers had an argument with some of the villagers. In the heat of the argument his co-worker said inadvertently: "If you don't believe in Jesus, there will be rain on the day of the idol parade." The villagers replied that if it did rain on that day they would go to the meetings. Later, when the incident was reported to Nee, he recognized the serious nature of the incident. There was hardly any sign

of rain in the near future. They all stopped their visitation
work and prayed earnestly for rain. Rain did come just
before the parade! Since it was only a light shower, the
villagers decided to carry the idol out anyway, believing
that surely he would stop the rain. Then came the down-
pour. Within a short distance three of the coolies stum-
bled and fell on the slippery ground, and the idol's jaw
and left arm were broken. So they took him inside and
made emergency repairs, and postponed the parade for
two days. Nee and his workers prayed again. Once more
it was a perfect day. But when the parade began, again
torrential rain struck. As a result the villagers were convinced that Jesus is the true God. Crowds came to a
saving knowledge of Christ.

Although in many ways a spiritual giant and a man used
by God, Nee is not without shortcomings and failures.
The most obvious and harmful to his ministry was the
operation of a pharmaceutical factory named "The China
Biological and Chemical Laboratories" (生化藥廠). It
was originally owned by his younger brother, who was
an accomplished chemistry professor. Too much
interested in research, he did not do well as a businessman.
Watchman Nee had long held the idea that there were
two Biblical ways for a preacher to obtain support: relying
entirely on the children of God to support him, or working
for his support during his spare time, like Paul's tent-
making. He therefore considered the operation of the
pharmaceutical factory to be a good means for meeting
the financial needs of his church and his co-workers. With
this in mind he took over the management of the factory
in 1942. Little did he know at the time that it was going
to be a hindrance to his ministry. Also, before long there
were many other church leaders in the "Little Flock"
movement who followed Nee in the practice of running

businesses to support their work and fellow, workers. Nee himself became so involved in business that for a long period of time after 1945 he could hardly find time for preaching. Nee struggled with this dilemma for a long time, until finally in 1948 he admitted his mistake in running the pharmaceutical factory, devoted himself entirely to the work of God, and dedicated his factory to the church. This brought a great revival among the "Little Flock" as other church leaders followed Nee in giving their businesses to the church. The church suddenly became very wealthy as the owner of businesses. Some of the money was used to purchase a large mansion in Shanghai for the training of workers. Another training center was also started in Kuling, Fuchow.

After 1948 it was also obvious that Nee did many things not consistent with what he had advocated in *Rethinking Our Missions.* For example, he had insisted in his book that it was wrong for churches to operate institutions such as schools or hospitals. However, it could be done by individual Christians. But in 1948, as the result of the revival, the church became the owner and manager of many different kinds of businesses. This was much worse than running orphanages and schools.

A more serious contradiction of his own principles was the fact that in his later practice he sent out workers (called "apostles"—those who got out to preach the gospel and set up churches from place to place in the "Little Flock" church) from one single place, which became a central training center and a headquarters for workers, instead of having them dispersed from existing churches all over the country as he advocated in his book. To account for the change of policy after 1948, an appendix was added in the 1966 edition of *Rethinking Our Missions.*

The establishment of this training center also resulted

in the division of workers into two classes, those who had been to the center and those who had not. The trained ones were given more power and authority. By doing this the "Little Flock" moved a great step towards denominational practices.

In *Rethinking Our Missions* Nee also held the idea that the worker (apostle) could never interfere with the internal affairs of the local church, which must be left to the elders to manage. However, after 1948 he both advocated and practiced the takeover and supervision of local churches. This caused a great schism in the local church in Fuchow, which already had two separate assemblies, only one of which was at this point recognized by Nee.

In 1949 when the Commuunists took over mainland China, Nee left his country to live in Hong Kong. However in 1950, when he learned of difficulties in his church in Shanghai, he went back without hesitation, knowing full well the great danger confronting him on his return.

As the leader of the largest group of Christians in China, Watchman Nee quickly came under the fierce purges of the early years of the Communist regime. During the Five-Anti campaign in 1952 he was accused of being a capitalist because of the fact that he had owned and operated a pharmaceutical factory, and was sentenced to fifteen years imprisonment.[2]

In 1956 the government began a major offensive against the "Little Flock," which had at the time numerous assemblies throughout the country. Church leaders in the Shanghai area were arrested. A mass denunciation meeting was called on January 30, to accomplish the rooting

---

[2]Leslie T. Lyall, *Come Wind, Come Weather* (Chicago: Moody Press, 1960), p. 81.

out of "counter-revolutionaries" hidden within the "Little Flock." Nee was denounced and labeled an adulterer who had seduced more than one hundred women. The sins and crimes of Nee and his group were widely publicized. The "Little Flock" church crumbled under the rampageous attack of the people with strong government support. It was completely reorganized and formally joined the Three-Self Movement on April 15. (The Three-Self Movement was an attempt by the Communists to divorce the church from "imperialist" influence and to wed it to the state instead. The "Three-Self" stands for self-governing, self-supporting, and self-propagating. These were, of course, given a Communist twist to mean freedom from imperialist control, imperialist finance, and imperialist "poison.")

Although Watchman Nee himself was rendered inactive by the Communist government in China, his influence continues to be felt outside the country, both in many parts of Asia and in North America. God had used him to bring a different kind of revival to China, one that is deep-rooted spiritually, and lasting. This was achieved through his special emphasis on the doctrine of salvation and the doctrine of the church. Many have criticized Nee's doctrine of the church as being exclusive and erratic. This may be true; but when a certain view of the church has resulted in the founding of hundreds of churches in China and outside of China within a short period of four decades, it deserves our attention.

Chapter 2

INTRODUCTION TO ECCLESIOLOGY

The Importance of the Doctrine

Ecclesiology looms very large in the thinking of Watchman Nee and his associates. In their opinion, the sixteenth century Protestant Reformation has failed in that it has not gone far enough. The retention of certain Roman Catholic ecclesiastical ills, coupled with the schismatic havoc created by the new situation, has brought about utter confusion and spiritual lethargy in the Christian church. In a situation like this it behooves every churchman to look deep into the Biblical teaching of the church and go back to the practice of the early apostolic church. In view of this, Nee and his associates regard the correct understanding of the Biblical concept of the church to be of paramount importance.

Since for Nee and his group the present confusion in the church is a result in some cases of ignorance regarding Scriptural teachings on church matters, and willful disobedience of clear Biblical injunctions in others, a quick look both at what they think is wrong with the Protestant church in general and at what they consider their position to be within Christendom will help us to put ourselves in their shoes so as to understand why they consider a correct ecclesiology to be so important. In his preface to the section on the doctrine of the church in *The Ministry of the Word,* Witness Lee writes:

We feel that the doctrine of the church and the doctrine of the Kingdom of heaven are the two most important doctrines among these sixty topics. What God cares about most in this age is this matter of the church and the Kingdom of heaven. The church is used to usher in the Kingdom of heaven. The Kingdom of heaven is His goal, and the church is what He uses to reach this goal. The manifold blessings that He has bestowed on the church and all that He has done for the church, are all for the realization of the Kingdom of heaven. Today, all the beloved of God who have received light from Him must live in His church with this will of God in mind and help to bring in the Kingdom of heaven. Pray that we all are men after His own heart in this particular matter.[1]

One result of the Reformation was the breaking up of the Protestant segment of Christendom into growing numbers of sects and denominations. For Nee and his associates, this is a terrible sin. The Scripture explicitly condemns this sectarian fragmentation of the Christian fellowship (I Corinthians 1:12–17) and regards it as an activity of the flesh (Galatians 5:20). An understanding and practice of the Biblical principle of church unity, they feel, would be able to cure this illness. But the dissension is already too deep to be corrected within the Protestant church. The only hope is for all enlightened children of God to come out of "denominational churches" and return to a Biblical stand on the local church.[2] Nee's view on church unity will be discussed in the section on the unity of the church.[3]

Another deplorable feature of the Protestant church is the ministerial system with its resulting abuses. Nee

---

[1]Witness Lee, "The Doctrine of the Church," *The Ministry of the Word.* LVII–LXI (May–September 1956), p. 1031.

[2]Witness Lee, *Understanding the Church* (Taiwan: Gospel Book Room, 1961), p. 122.

[3]See pp. 66–77

considers this to be a return to the Roman Catholic priestly and mediatorial system, which is definitely against the New Testament teaching of the priesthood of all Christians. One result of this ministerial system is the peculiar type of Sunday service at which the minister speaks while the congregation listens. Moreover, the creation of such a hierarchy in the church has lead to passivity and non-involvement on the part of the laity in service and other spiritual matters, and has culminated in the existing great spiritual stagnation in the Protestant church. Nee in his *Rethinking Our Missions* laments the abuse of this Protestant priestly system and "solo" type of church meeting in these words of denunciation:

> Therefore the consequence of this confusion in the nature of our meetings is extremely serious. On the one hand, the brothers sink into spiritual passivity and apathy. On the other hand, the demand for workers to station in all these churches to take up preaching responsibilities hinders the rapid progress of the spread of the gospel, and deprives many a sinner of the opportunity to obtain salvation. The root of the problem is, of course, man's assumption that there has to be this kind of preaching meeting called the Sunday service. Who can preach better than God's workers? The workers, therefore, have to locate at one church to maintain this preaching meeting while the spreading of the gospel is neglected and sinners cannot be saved. But after all, has the local church been benefited? Not at all! The believer has become forever a listener in the work and not a brother in the church![4]

We will go into greater detail in these matters in our discussion on Nee's view of church organization and church worship.

Worst of all, there is a general disregard of the Biblical truth of the church. There has been little concern about the true nature of the church among the average Chris-

[4]Watchman Nee, *Rethinking Our Missions* (Taiwan: Gospel Book Room, 1966), p. 313.

tians. According to Witness Lee, this is the most neglected
area in the whole truth of God. In his book *The Vision
of the Building Up of the Church,* he writes:

> I have come to the realization these days that this matter
> of the building up of the church is by far the most neglected
> and confused question for the children of God. We have
> no problem with the other truths such as the gospel, the
> spiritual life, and Christ. But when it comes to the question
> of the tabernacle, that is, the church, many people become
> confused.[5]

Thus for Nee and Lee the Protestant church as a whole
is incorrigibly wrong. It has broken away from the Roman
Catholic Church in an attempt to revert back to the practice of the apostolic church; however, it has not quite
attained it. What we need is an understanding of the
true nature of the church and a willingness to follow
the example of the New Testament church. A full discussion of these topics must await later occasions. Suffice
it to say here that for Witness Lee the theme of the
entire Bible is the building of the church. In his book
The Vision of the Building Up of the Church, he labors
to show that from Genesis to Revelation the history of
the Bible is centered on the building of the tabernacle,
the temple, and the church. The history of the Old Testament describes the building of the tabernacle and the
temple, which are types of the New Testament church.
God's primary concern was that His people should build
the right tabernacle to house the ark which typifies Christ.
To neglect the building up of the church according to
the will of God is just like putting the ark in a wrong
place. In the pattern given to Moses, God certainly made
no provision for that to happen. And Old Testament history bears this out.

[5]Witness Lee, *The Vision of the Building Up of the Church* (Taiwan:
Gospel Book Room, 1964), p. 104.

Nee also points out that God's manifold blessings—the Holy Spirit, the light of God, and in particular the new life in Christ—are given to the church as a *whole,* although we usually put greater emphasis on the *individual's* spiritual life. But as a matter of fact, our Lord's life is in the church. In view of this, whether or not a certain group of people *is* the "church" becomes very important, for God has placed all spiritual blessings within the church.[6]

The importance of the doctrine of the church for Watchman Nee is best seen in his understanding of the world-wide Brethren Movement of the nineteenth century, and the position he assigns to it in the entire history of the church.

In his book *The Orthodox Tradition of the Church,* which is an exposition of the seven churches of the book of Revelation, Nee seeks to demonstrate that all seven churches belong to the prophetic future at the time of the writing of the Apocalypse, and that they could be divided into two groups: the first three belong to what is now historic past while the latter four, though emerging at different points in the history of the church, have all come into existence and will continue, all four of them, until the Second Advent of our Lord. The first two, Ephesus and Smyrna, followed the apostolic tradition and remained in the orthodox position. But during the period represented by Pergamos, the church began to depart from the apostolic tradition. Thyatira (the Roman Catholic Church) followed the devious path of Pergamos and will exist until the Second Coming. Sardis (the Protestant church), coming out of the Roman Catholic Church, attempts to revert to the old apostolic tradition. But it did not completely revert to type. Sardis, too, will exist until the Second Coming. Then in the nineteenth century

[6]Watchman Nee, *The Way of the Church* (Hong Kong: Hong Kong Gospel Book Room, 1951), p. 1.

there emerged the Brethren Movement which is represented by the Philadelphia church. Dissatisfied with the Reformation Movement, they came out of it and succeeded in going back to the apostolic orthodox tradition. However, not all the Brethren stayed pure and irreproachable. Some of them took pride in their spiritual and material wealth and departed from the Philadelphia position. Nee says these people are represented by the Laodicean church, the "proud, fallen Philadelphians."[7] The seven churches of Revelation, which speak of the development of the church throughout history, are represented by the following diagram.[8]

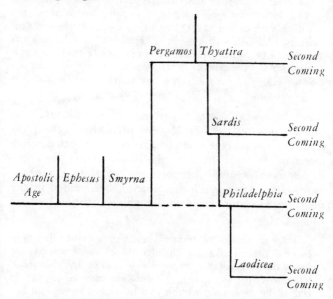

[7]Watchman Nee, *The Orthodox Tradition of the Church* (Taiwan: Gospel Book Room, 1963), p. 75.
[8]*Ibid*, p. 52.

Thus we can see how Nee views the importance of the Brethren Movement in light of the teaching of the book of Revelation. He hails it as far more important than the Reformation of the sixteenth century:

> This movement is far greater than the Reformation Movement. I must say that the work of Philadelphia is more important than the Reformation. What Philadelphia has given us is what we did not get from the Reformation. We thank God that the Brethren Movement has solved the question of the church. The position of God's children has also been recovered. Therefore we see that both in quality and quantity the Brethren Movement has surpassed the Reformation. . . . From that time on people began to understand the true nature of the church, realizing that it is the body of Christ. All God's children belong to one church, which is indivisible. What becomes important for them are the brethren and the genuine love for each other that they display. Jesus said, "There will come out a church whose name is Philadelphia."[9]

But how was Nee to relate himself and his group to this world-wide Brethren Movement? This was the question confronting Nee when he first heard of such a movement, in 1927. At that time the first question that arose in his mind was whether or not they should join the movement. After much deliberation he decided in the negative. He later reviewed the whole situation in these important words:

> It was not until 1927 that we began to learn of this movement in other countries. Through books and magazines we found that it is a large movement which has made its influence felt all over the world, just like the Reformation Movement. But at the same time we felt that many had fallen into the position of Laodicea. At that time a question arose in our mind: What does the Bible say? Are the children of God

[9]*Ibid.*, pp. 61, 62.

supposed to join a movement? The unity of Christians should be in Christ and not in a movement. This led us to search deeper into the Scriptures until we became more and more convinced that whatever is larger or smaller than a local church cannot be called a church. God has revealed to us that there are four different groups in His church. Perhaps we could say that there is the Roman Church, the Reformation Church, the Brethren, and the Brethren Church. The fourth church, the Brethren Church, has already fallen into the position of Laodicea. That organization has already become a denomination. Once I asked a brother: "Do you think I look like a brother?" He replied, "You look like one, all right, but among 'you' there is still. . . ." Immediately I cut him short by saying "What do you mean by this 'you'? Is it not enough that I became a brother? 'We' includes all those redeemed by the blood." Any time a brother is saved in Chungking and the church in Chungking still says he is not a brother, then the church in Chungking has become a denomination. If you require him to have something more beside being a brother before you are willing to call him a brother, then it becomes denominationalism. Although these people do not call themselves the Brethren denomination they have already built an invisible wall around themselves.[10]

These words of Nee not only give us his view of the Brethren Movement but also reveal to us how important it is to those of the "Little Flock" that they hold a right view of the doctrine of the church. To have a wrong concept of the church and build accordingly is to build a temple not according to the divine blueprint. Moreover, it has taken the church over a thousand years to arrive at the correct idea of the local church, which is the only way to church unity. Nee concludes, therefore, that we must hold on to it and carry it out in practice. This results in the ostracism of Nee and his group from all denominational churches. The tension created also moves Nee and his followers to keep refining their ecclesiology.

[10]*Ibid.*, p. 85.

The Approach to the Doctrine

Nee has a very high view of the inspiration and authority of the Bible. We can be sure that he believes in its plenary inspiration and inerrancy. The Bible is for him the authoritative guide in matters of faith and practice. His books and messages are all based on these presuppositions. Thus it is only natural that his treatment of ecclesiology has a Biblical approach. His loud cry for the return to apostolic practices demands in particular that he follow the Bible very closely in his treatment of the doctrine.

According to him, God never leaves any divine work to human imagination.[11] He has already set a heavenly pattern for us in Scripture concerning church formation and organization. All we need do is to look into the Bible and find out this pattern, and then follow it.[12]

His approach is also historical. In his *Normal Christian Church Life,* where he treats the subject of the missionary activities of church planting and church organization, he takes as a starting point the commission of Paul in Antioch to take the gospel to other lands. Then he follows Paul's journey and points out different principles of the work of the apostle in establishing churches and appointing elders. Historical examples are very important for him. It is God's will that we should learn from the experiences of these men in the Bible. He explains this in these words:

> Christianity is built not only upon precepts but also upon examples. God has revealed His will not only by giving orders but by having certain things done in His Church, so that in the ages to come others might simply look at the pattern and know His will. God has directed His people not only by means of abstract principles and objective regulations but

[11] Watchman Nee, *The Normal Christian Church Life* (Washington, D.C.: International Students Press, 1962), p. 10.
[12] *Ibid.*

by concrete examples and subjective experience. God does use precepts to teach His people, but one of His chief methods of instruction is through history. God tells us how others knew and did His will, so that we by looking at their lives may not only know His will but see how to do it, too. He worked in their lives, producing in them what He Himself desired, and He bids us look at them so that we may know what He is after.[13]

Both Nee and Lee are fond of the allegorical approach in the interpretation of the Bible. Lee, in comparison, is much more dependent than Nee on this approach to the understanding of God's Word. For him, everything in the material realm has a corresponding reality in the spiritual sphere. He even goes to the extent of making a statement like this: "In today's universe all the material symbolizes the spiritual."[14]

One example of Lee's extreme way of spiritualizing Scripture is found in his exposition of the first two chapters of Genesis, where he attempts to find a type of the church in Eve.[15] According to him, in the first two chapters of the first book of the Bible we find God taking four steps in building up a true church. The first step is the creation of man from the dust of the earth. God breathed His spirit into the man and made him a living soul with a spirit which enabled him to have direct communication with Him. The second step is putting man in front of the tree of life. This tree symbolizes God, who makes Himself available to us in receivable form so that we can partake of His life (John 6). All this is used to bring out the New Testament truth of regeneration. Thirdly, there is the description of the rivers running through the garden, laying bare the gold, bdellium, and onyx stone. This symbolizes the fact that after God's life has entered

[13]*Ibid.*, p. 11.
[14]Lee, *The Vision of the Building Up of the Church*. p 20.
[15]*Ibid.*, pp. 29–34.

ours, it moves and works in us to produce God's nature represented by the gold, and a transformed personality which is represented by the bdellium and onyx stone. Then, fourthly, we come to the end of the second chapter where we see God putting these glorious materials (transformed men) together to make a bride. This passage speaks of the creation of Eve, a creature coming out of Adam to become his bride. Thus the building of the church—a universal bride for the universal Bridegroom—is accomplished.

This way of allegorizing Scripture leads both Nee and Lee to see many types of the New Testament church in the Bible. They hold that the glorious church of God is represented in the Bible by four women: Eve, the wife in Ephesians 5, the woman of Revelation 12, and the Lamb's bride (who is the New Jerusalem) in Revelation 21.[16] Of equal importance as types of the church are the Old Testament tabernacle and temple.[17] We will go into detailed discussion of these types when we come to the section on the nature of the church.

Finally, it must be pointed out that Nee is very much against systematic treatment of the truth of God. Ten years after his conversion he produced a three volume closely-reasoned systematic treatment of the three constituent parts of man, the body, soul, and spirit, entitled *The Spiritual Man.* Later he regretted very much having written this dogmatic treatment of the truth of God in such a systematic, organized fashion. He had this to say some twenty years ago in connection with the writing of *The Spiritual Man:*

> Some years back I was very ill, and the doctor said I could only live a few months. In the face of this I felt burdened

---

[16]Witness Lee, *The Glorious Church* (Hong Kong: Hong Kong Gospel Book Room, 1953), pp. 1,2.
[17]Lee, *The Vision of the Building Up of the Church,* pp. 41–44.

to write down in book form what the Lord had shown me on the subject of "the spiritual man," and thus to share with others the light I had been given. I did so and it was published, and the edition is now exhausted. It will not be reprinted.[18] It was not that what I wrote was wrong, for as I read it now I can endorse it all. It was a very clear and complete setting forth of the truth. But just there lies its weakness. It is *too* good, and it is the illusion of perfectness about it that troubles me. The headings, the orderliness, the systematic way in which the subject is worked out, the logic of the argument—all are too perfect to be spiritual. They lend themselves too easily to a merely mental apprehension. When a man has read the book he ought not to have any questions left; they ought all to be answered!

But God, I have discovered, does not do things that way, and much less does He let *us* do them. We human beings are not to produce "perfect" books. The danger of such perfection is that a man can understand without the help of the Holy Spirit. But if God gives us books they will ever be broken fragments, not always clear or consistent or logical, lacking conclusions, and yet coming to us in life and ministering life to us. We cannot dissect divine facts and outline and systematize them. It is only the immature Christian who demands always to have intellectually satisfying conclusions. The Word of God itself has this fundamental character, that it speaks always and essentially to our spirit and to our life.[19]

From this it is clear that Nee does not prize the systematic treatment of the doctrine of the church or any other doctrine very highly. The above words also enable us to gain an insight into his approach to all the truth of God, and even to his entire ministry.

Witness Lee, on the other hand, does follow a systematic approach to the treatment of divine truth. In his volumes on important doctrines, which were first published as

[18]This was subsequently reissued in Chinese in 1964 and published in English in 1968.

[19]Watchman Nee, *What Shall this Man Do?* (Fort Washington, Pennsylvania: Christian Literature Crusade, 1967), pp. 7,8.

articles in the magazine *The Ministry of the Word,* Lee
demonstrates great interest in the orderly topical treatment of God's Word. A certain doctrine is studied point
after point. He begins each point by citing pertinent texts
and then explains what they mean. As far as the format
of these volumes is concerned, they appear to be little
more than an annotated topical arrangement of scriptures.
Even so, it could be said that Lee has descended to what
Nee calls the substitution of the ministering of the dead
letter for the ministering of life and spirit.

The Word *Ekklesia*—"Church"

The Greek word *ekklesia*—from which, via the Latin,
we obtain our English word "ecclesiology"—sheds much
light on the meaning and nature of the church. Nee and
his associates are therefore careful in investigating the
meaning and the usage of the word in the Bible. Nee's
investigation leads him to the conclusion that the word
as first used in Acts does not imply the idea of organized
believers. It is used simply to designate a group of people
who were saved by the gospel of Jesus Christ.[20] The
word *ekklesia* appears only three times in the four Gospels. The book of Acts uses the same word twenty times.
The book does not, however, begin by telling us how
the saved were organized. It starts by telling us that a
crowd of three thousand, and then another five thousand,
came to the Lord, without describing explicitly how they
organized themselves into a church. Then in chapter five
they were suddenly called "the church." This is the first
use of the word in Acts.[21] Soon after, in chapter eight,

[20]Nee, *Rethinking Our Missions.* p. 152.
[21]In Acts 2:47, the word *ekklesia* is not found in the best Greek
texts.

we are told that the church in Jerusalem was persecuted. At this point we begin to understand the meaning of the word "church." A church is simply a group of saved people at a certain place. Later we see Paul going out on his missionary journeys. People were saved, but, says Nee, Paul did not establish organized churches of new converts. Thus it is clear that wherever a group of people were saved, they *automatically* constituted a church. We do not find any particular procedures that the apostles used to organize a group of people into a church. Nee states the result of his findings in these words:

> The groups of believers in these different places are called churches, without any explanation whatever as to how they came to be churches.[22]

It must be immediately pointed out, however, that Nee is not against church organization and government. We shall see, as we come to these topics later, that he is very much interested in church polity. What he is driving at is that the word "church" is basically used to designate a group of believers, regardless of organization.

Witness Lee, who is always more systematic in his treatment of Biblical doctrines, defines *ekklesia* this way:

> In Greek, church (see Matthew 16:18; 18:17) is *ekklesia*. It is a combination of two words, *ek* meaning coming out, and *klesia* meaning those who are called. So the meaning of the word is the called-out ones or the assembly of those called out. "Church" means a group of people called out of the world by God and gathered together.[23]

Lee also makes the point that although the Old Testament does not mention the church explicitly, there is a good picture of the concept of the church in the story of the exodus.[24] Having come out of Egypt, the Hebrews

---

[22]Nee, *The Normal Christian Church Life*, p. 58.
[23]Lee, *Understanding the Church*. p. 3.   [24]*Ibid.*, pp. 3,4.

organized themselves after the pattern specified by God
at the foot of Mount Sinai. The New Testament calls
them an *ekklesia* (Acts 7:38). This group of people called
by God out of Egypt and assembled together suggests
to us the idea of a New Testament church.

The word "church," according to Lee, could not be
used to denote a building, as it is so often wrongly used.
The Bible says that a church can fear and pray (Acts
5:11, 12:5), so it must be a living thing and not a material
building.[25] Neither could the word be used for a church
organization, such as a mission, an evangelistic agency,
or a denomination. The church, in the Biblical sense,
is a body and an organism (Ephesians 1:23, Colossians
1:18).

The Twofold Aspect: Universal and Local

Because of their emphasis on the local church and their
denunciation of the disunity of the Protestant church,
Nee and his associates are very careful in defining the
relationship between the universal and local church. Nee
makes clear distinction between the universal and the
local. Lee, on the other hand, while not going to the
extreme of saying that there is no universal or invisible
church, tries his best to minimize the importance of the
concept of the universal church. If he does not say that
there is no distinction between the universal and the local
church, he has at least made statements to the effect that
the two are almost identical. He points out that there
is no such a term as the "universal church" in the Bible.[26]
Moreover, the church appears as local churches on this
earth, first in Jerusalem and then in other places. But

[25]*Ibid.*, pp. 1,2.   [26]*Ibid.*, p. 19.

of course, says Lee, if the church appears in Jerusalem, it also appears in the universe. Just as there is one universal church, there should be only one local church at one locality, because the latter is an expression in concrete form of the former, it being only an abstract concept. Lee puts it this way:

> The church must appear on earth so that it could appear in the universe. Therefore we cannot speak of the church without locality. Once we take the church out of its locality, then it has no existence in the universe. Away from the confines of locality, the concept of church is only empty talk. There is no church in the universe if there is no local church. We recognize the nature of the church to be universal, and also its existence in the universe. Yet we must also realize that its story in the universe was told only through its appearance on earth. Therefore, no locality, no church.[27]

Lee also gives three reasons for the importance of the local church which is the actualization of the universal church.[28] These also help us to understand the relationship between the two. First of all, he points out that the establishment of the universal church is through the local church. Or in other words, the establishment of the local church is the establishment of the universal church. Secondly, it is only obvious that the universal church requires the local church to carry out her government and administration. Thirdly, for both the worker and the layman the universal church is only an abstract concept. Only the local church is real to them. This becomes clear when one considers the fact that all the work of the local workers is done in and for the local church, and that both the fellowship and service of all believers also take place within the local church. It is apparent, then, that to Lee the local church is far more significant than the universal church.

---

[27]*Ibid*., pp. 23,24.   [28]*Ibid*., pp. 26–31.

Nee, on the other hand, approaches the question of the twofold aspect of the church from another angle. For him there is the outward form of Christianity as well as the inward reality. For instance, very often we see only the outward forms of a certain truth and our carnal minds adopt extreme views on divine things. Thus we attempt to differentiate between the outward ceremony of baptism and its spiritual significance. In like manner we recognize both a material and spiritual level when dealing with the elements of the Lord's supper. But as a matter of fact the Bible makes no such differences. It states only one divine truth. Following the same line of thought, he has this to say about the so-called institutionalized church and the true universal church.

> But what we have just said about the reality of Baptism and the Lord's Table is no less true when we come to speak of the reality of the Church. . . . Care is exercised to differentiate between the true Church and the false. But in the Lord's Word, and in the thought of God, there is no such distinction. The Lord put no footnote in Scripture when He spoke of the Church. He did not seek to safeguard the spiritual reality by differentiating between an inward and outward, a real and an unreal. He did not even draw a clear line of demarcation between the local and the universal. In the Word of God there is only 'the Church'.[29]

In other words, Nee is saying that there is the distinction between the local and universal church only when we view things from a materialistic and intellectual point of view, which we are not supposed to do. But when we view things from God's standpoint, then we shall see only one church, as God does.

Unwilling as Nee and Lee are to stress a clear-cut difference between the universal and the local church, yet Scriptural evidence is simply too strong for men like them,

---

[29]Nee, *What Shall this Man Do?*, pp. 164,165.

who have the highest respect for the inspired Word of God, to completely ignore the necessity of a distinction. So Nee defines the twofold nature of the church in these words:

> We have clearly two different aspects of the Church before us—the Church and the churches, the universal Church and the local churches. The Church is invisible; the churches are visible. The Church has no organization; the churches are organized. The Church is spiritual; the churches are spiritual and yet physical. The Church is purely an organism; the churches are an organism, yet at the same time they are organized, which is seen by the fact that elders and deacons hold office there.[30]

In the following two chapters we shall examine the nature and functions of the universal church and the local church in detail.

[30]Nee, *The Normal Christian Church Life*, p. 46.

Chapter 3

THE CHURCH UNIVERSAL

The Foundation of the Church

In his discussion on the foundation of the church, Nee takes up Peter's confession in Matthew 16 to show that the rock on which the church was built is "a confession based upon a revelation of a Person."[1]

Peter's confession is one not only of Jesus' person but also of His office and ministry. This dual discovery also becomes Paul's starting point in all his writings. For example, in Romans he begins his doctrinal discourse with these words:

> Concerning his Son Jesus Christ our Lord, which was made of the seed of David according to the flesh; and declared to be the Son of God with power, according to the spirit of holiness, by the resurrection from the dead.[2]

In Nee's own words, Christ as the foundation of God's church is all important:

> All God's purpose, all God's hopes are bound up with that risen Christ. It is He who has been separated and anointed as God's sure foundation.[3]

It is also important that we understand this Christ as a "revealed" Christ and not a doctrinal or theoretical Christ of mere head knowledge. Even a year-long study

[1] Watchman Nee, *What Shall this Man Do?*, pp. 70–74.
[2] Romans 1:3,4.   [3] Nee, *loc. cit.* p. 72.

of theology cannot build us into His church. This knowledge is an inner knowledge coming from God's direct revelation in the individual's heart. A mere possession of head knowledge—a knowledge of doctrine and theology—cannot prevail against the gates of hell. A true knowledge of Christ comes only from God's revelation. Nee puts it this way:

> This revelation is Christianity. There is no Church without it. I, from within, recognize Jesus as Son of God, and as Christ—that is the heart of everything. The response of Jesus to Peter was not 'You have answered correctly' but 'God has shown that to you!'[4]

This true knowledge that we have of Christ should be confessed in public. The church is founded not only on revelation, but also on confession. God likes for us to speak out this "thou art"; doing so makes hell fear.

To sum up, Nee sees that the church is founded on the person and work of Christ, which is revealed to individuals who then, with their confession of this revealed knowledge, become the living stones used to build the house of God.

Both Nee and Lee recognize that the church is heavenly in its true characteristic and is thus an eternal entity. God planned it in the eternal past, as Ephesians 3:10,11 reveals. Thus the idea was in God's mind even before the creation of the earth.[5] Lee believes that the church began at Pentecost and was a mystery to the Old Testament saints. However, there are many allusions to the church in the Old Testament in the form of types. The first of these is Eve. We have already looked at how he arrived at this conclusion in connection with the discussion on his allegorical approach to the doctrine.[6] What

[4]Ibid., p. 74.
[5]Witness Lee, "The Doctrine of the Church," The Ministry of the Word, LVII–LXI (May–September, 1956), p. 1031.
[6]See pp. 36–40.

should be added here is Lee's theory of the non-redemptive death of Christ that he holds in connection with Eve as a type of the church.[7]

In Lee's typological interpretation, Adam signifies Christ. Eve was formed out of Adam in his sleep. Likewise, the church also came out of Christ. Adam's sleep corresponds to Christ's unredemptive death. There are two aspects to Christ's death: one is His atonement for sin, and one is the release of His own life to form the church. This is clear when we remember that Adam's sleep was not for the redemption of Eve, who at that time was sinless, but for the extraction of a piece of bone to make Eve. The blood and water which came out of Jesus' side on the cross, according to Lee, also supports this theory. The blood is for redemption, but the water, a symbol of life, is for the formation of His church. Lee also notices that in Genesis 2:22,23, Eve is spoken of as bone of Adam's bones and flesh of his flesh. No mention is made of blood. In other places man is spoken of as flesh and blood (Matthew 16:17, I Corinthians 15:50). Only the resurrected body is flesh and bones (Luke 24:39). Here is another piece of evidence that Genesis 2 has nothing to do with redemption. It is a clear picture of the unblemished church in God's eternal plan.

The New Testament church in the Old Testament is also represented by other women, each of whom prefigures certain aspects of the church's relationship with Christ. How Rebecca was given to Isaac portrays how the church was presented to Christ. The joining of hands in marriage of Joseph and Asenath in Egypt depicts how the church was chosen and called out of the world to belong to God. Zipporah's marriage to Moses is a picture of the church in the wilderness. In the book of Joshua

---

[7]Witness Lee, *The Glorious Church* (Hong Kong: Hong Kong Gospel Book Room, 1953), pp. 35–42.

we have Achsah, who right after her marriage to Othniel requested of her father both the upper and lower springs —which describe the church's portion of inheritance. Ruth is a type of the redeemed church. Finally, Abigail, wife of David, is a type of the church militant. Although they all are used to describe certain aspects of the New Testament church, there is a major difference between Eve and these other women as types of the church. She is a type of the church before the Fall, while the others are figures of the church after the Fall.

More important as types of the church, according to Lee, are the tabernacle and the temple. In Lee's allegorical scheme, everything in the tabernacle has a parallel in the New Testament church. The brass altar symbolizes the judgment of God, for the brass came from the censers of the two hundred and fifty rebels who received the judgment of fire (Numbers 16). At the same time the altar also implies redemption and consecration. In the spiritual realm the altar thus speaks of a Christian's first step taken in his heavenly pilgrimage. After the experience of the altar we come to that of the laver, which signifies the illumination of the Holy Spirit and His work of regeneration as referred to in Titus 3:5. Next is the hanging for the court. The brass sockets similarly speak of the judgment of the cross. Silver in the Bible represents redemption; thus the silver hooks and fillets mean that those who received the judgment of the cross are those who are redeemed. After the washing of regeneration by the Holy Spirit and the dealing of the cross, a person acquires a garment of righteousness before God; and this is represented by the fine twined linen. The whole hanging signifies a Christian's life of separation from this world.

Passing through the outer court we come into the tent. In the tent there are two objects. The first is the ark of testimony, which is made of wood and gold. The ark of testimony is a symbol of Christ. The gold represents the nature of God and the wood represents the nature of man, thus the two natures of Christ. After having received the life of Christ we need spiritual nourishment from heaven, and this is represented by the showbread. Having feasted on the heavenly bread of our Lord we are able to shine with the light of life. This is symbolized by the candlestick. All these spiritual experiences produce in a Christian a sense of satisfaction which prompts him to offer prayers and praise, thanksgiving and adoration. This is indicated by the burnt sweet incense. But it is not enough for *individual* Christians to have the perfect spiritual life. There must also be the tent itself. It will not do to have all the inside objects without the tent itself, and the tent is a type of the church. It is an expansion of the ark, meaning that the church is an expanded Christ. The boards that made up the sides of the tent speak of individual Christians. These boards were each a cubit and a half wide, i.e., half of three cubits—three being the number for building up. This means that to built up the church, a single Christians will not do. We all need each other for the building up of God's church.[8]

It is in this manner that Lee sees the full significance of a New Testament church in the tabernacle. The temple is only an enlargement of the tabernacle and thus has the same significance.

The Establishment of the Church

As mentioned before, Lee holds that the church was an eternal heavenly entity planned by God before the

---

[8]One should realize, of course, that this typological analysis of the tabernacle is not original with Lee, or Nee either, but has been set forth in most of its details by various Brethren writers—and, undoubtedly, by others before them. The idea of taking the tent as representative of the church, however, seems to belong to Lee.

creation of heaven and earth in the eternal past. Yet from the human point of view it was a mystery to the Old Testament saints. Pentecost marked the actual beginning of the church. Though the first mention of the church was made in Matthew 16, where Jesus says that He will build His church (Matthew 16:18), the use of the future tense indicates that the church was not in existence at that time. In Matthew 18 Jesus speaks of church discipline, indicating that the establishment of the church is at hand and that they should bring matters to the church which they could not solve among themselves.[9]

On the day of Pentecost the Holy Spirit descended and the church was officially inaugurated. The Bible says that after this event saved souls were added to the church daily (Acts 2:47).[10] The saved were also called "the church" in Acts 5:11. Theologically speaking, it is a fact that the church could not have existed before Pentecost. Jesus had not been crucified, raised from the dead, and exalted to His position in heaven. In other words, the church's foundation in redemption had not been accomplished. Moreover, the Holy Spirit had not yet come. Without Christ, the cross, and the Holy Spirit there could be no church. The church was established by the apostles' preaching about Christ's redemptive ministry and by the working of the transforming power of the Holy Spirit.[11]

Some think that Jesus had no intention of establishing a church. For Lee, He not only had full intention of founding the church, He was also actually the founder of the church.[12] In His first mention of the church, in Matthew 16, Christ makes it clear that He is not only the source and foundation of the church, He is also the founder

---

[9]Lee, *The Ministry of the Word*, LVII–LXI, p. 1037.
[10]Technically Lee is in error here, because *ekklesia* (church) does not appear in the best Greek texts.
[11]*Ibid.*, p. 1039.
[12]*Ibid.*

of it. "Upon this rock I will build my church," says Jesus
(Matthew 16:18). The book of Acts also declares that
it was the Lord who added converts to the church (Acts
2:47).[10] So, though on the human level it was the apostles
and early Christians who evangelized and showed people
the way to the Kingdom, it was actually the Lord who
accomplished all this through the Holy Spirit. Paul also
tells us that God was the one who "tempered the body,"
that is, the church, together (I Corinthians 12:24). Then
again in I Corinthians 3:9, Ephesians 2:22, and I Peter
2:4–6 it is said that God builds the church. Thus the
establishing and building up of the church is the work
of God in Christ through the Holy Spirit.

Not only had Christ the intention of founding a church,
He also took steps to realize His intention. The calling
of the twelve apostles was to train them for the ministry
of establishing the church. Watchman Nee has written
a book called *What Shall This Man Do?* It is a study
of the three distinct ministries of Peter, Paul, and John.
He summarizes the theme of his book in these words:

> So we have before us three representative men. We have
> Peter, concerned first with the ingathering of souls; we have
> Paul, the wise master-builder, building according to the
> heavenly vision given to him; and then, when failure threatens,
> we have John introduced to reaffirm that there is an original
> purpose still in view, and one that, in the mind of God,
> has never been abandoned. There is still something which
> He intends to fulfil, and from that intention He will never
> be deflected.[13]

The definite ministry which each of these three men
carried out was interestingly connected with the kind of
occupation which he had before Christ called him. Peter
was a fisherman. So he became a fisher of men, one who
was used by God to bring men in great numbers into

[13]Nee, *What Shall this Man Do?*, pp. 17,18.

the church. Paul, a tent-maker, wove the sheet of Peter's vision into a tent. He constructed what Peter initiated. John, who was mending his net when he was called, was commissioned to restore damage done to the early church.

Thus we see how the founder of the church was careful in choosing His men to prepare them for the building up of His church. It requires these three complementary and interrelating ministries to construct a perfect church.

No doubt Peter occupied a special position as an instrument of God in the establishment of the church. To him were given the keys to the Kingdom. There have been great controversies, not just between Catholics and Protestants but among Protestant theologians themselves, over the meaning of Peter's keys. Nee's understanding of the meaning of the keys is like this:

> A key implies, among other things, an entry, a beginning. You come in by a door, and you use a key for opening it, or for letting others in. In the outcome, Peter's ministry often issued in such a beginning of things, and his was in fact the first to do so. The Church in Jerusalem began when three thousand souls received his word, and the Church in Caesarea began when, in his presence, the Holy Spirit fell on Cornelius and his household. Thus we may say that, when Peter stood up with the eleven, he opened the door to the Jews, and when later he preached Christ in the Roman home, he opened it again to the Gentiles. So although on neither occasion Peter was alone, for the commission extends always to others beside him, and although later on we find that Paul too was a man chosen of God to have a still wider ministry of the gospel among the Gentiles, yet in a true sense Peter was the pioneer. Historically he held the key and he opened the door. His task was to initiate something. He was ordained by God to make the beginnings.[14]

The gospel of the ministry of Christ, especially His redemptive work on the cross, was used by Peter and

[14]*Ibid.*, p. 11.

the early apostles in ushering people into the Kingdom of God. We have already noticed Witness Lee's teaching on the importance of Christ, the cross, and the Holy Spirit in the founding of the church. Nee, in his treatment of the relationship between the redemptive work of Christ and the church, His body, singles out the cross from the other aspects of Christ's redemptive work. In his opinion, the cross is "the only gateway into this fellowship with one another in Jesus Christ."[15] This simply means that, subjectively speaking, when one becomes a Christian his old man is crucified with Christ, and he is brought into union with the risen and ascended life of Christ. The cross is therefore of pivotal importance in the founding of the church.

The Church and the Kingdom

Both Watchman Nee and Witness Lee have much to say about the relationship between the Kingdom of God and the church. Nee defines the Kingdom of God as the sovereignty (kingship) of God.[16] Wherever the sovereignty of God holds full sway, there is the Kingdom of God. Revelation 12:10 says that the coming of the Kingdom of God is the coming of the sovereignty of Christ. The extent of sovereign rule defines the limits of the Kingdom. When Christ said that the Kingdom of God was in the midst of the Jews, He did not mean in the hearts of men. He simply meant that *He* was in their midst. Christ submitted Himself entirely to the sovereign will and rule of God; thus He was and is the embodiment of the Kingdom of God.

The eternal purpose of God is to prepare for Himself

[15]*Ibid.,* p. 68.

[16]Watchman Nee, *Authority and Obedience* (Taiwan: Gospel Book Room, 1967), p. 49.

a Kingdom where He can exercise His sovereign rule
and manifest His glory. The universe was created for
this purpose. Yet both Satan and Adam disrupted this
divine plan. The history of the Bible throughout is God's
work in the restoration of His Kingdom.

After the Fall of Adam, God chose Noah to obey His
rule, and He gave men the power of self-government.
But this self-rule soon became corrupted, culminating
in the Babel rebellion which was a challenge to the rule
of God. Later God chose Abraham to establish His Kingdom on earth. Unfortunately, soon thereafter all of
Abraham's descendants went to Egypt and fell under the
rule of Pharaoh. God brought them out of Egypt and
established them in Canaan. There they became dissatisfied with the theocratic system that God had set up
for them and demanded the rule of a king. Even so, God
found in King David a man after His own heart and was
able through him to carry out His rule. But after David
corruption soon prevailed and God again lost His kingly
rule on earth when Israel was captured by Babylon. God
did not recover His sovereign rule until the coming of
Christ, whose redemptive work brought a people out
of the Satanic rule. His Kingdom was once again established on this earth when the church was founded.
Nevertheless, the church as the realm of God's kingly
rule on earth did not last long. It became corrupted. God
remedied this situation by calling some Christians to
become overcomers. These are the children of God who
will rule with Christ in the millennium and in eternity.

Lee's view differs somewhat from Nee's. It is at the
point of difference between the Kingdom of God and
the Kingdom of heaven that Witness Lee has become
very emphatic. He believes that the Kingdom of God
is the realm of God's sovereign rule. Wherever the existence of God is, there is His Kingdom—whether God's
full sway is evident there or not; and since the existence

of God is from eternity to eternity, therefore His Kingdom also extends from eternity to eternity. It includes
the eternity before the creation of this universe, the Garden of Eden and the chosen patriarchs, the nation of
Israel of the Old Testament, the church of today, the
millennial Kingdom and the Kingdom of heaven, and
the new heaven and new earth which will last forever.[17]

The Kingdom of heaven, on the other hand, is within
the Kingdom of God but not identical with it. It began
when the New Testament church began at Pentecost.
When Christ was on earth He declared that the Kingdom
of heaven was at hand, which means that it had not yet
come. Besides, the words of Jesus in Matthew 21:43
indicate that it was the Kingdom of God and not the
Kingdom of heaven which was in their midst. We see
in Matthew 22:2–4 that, after Christ's death and redemptive work was accomplished, the Kingdom of
heaven began with the preaching of the gospel. The pro-
clamation that the Kingdom of heaven was at hand also
shows—Lee stresses—that, unlike the Kingdom of God,
it did have a beginning. Again in Matthew 16:18, 19,
our Lord, after declaring that He will build His church,
states that He will give to Peter the keys of the Kingdom
of heaven. Thus when Peter used the key at Pentecost,
that was the beginning of the Kingdom of heaven.

However, the Kingdom of heaven is not identical with
the church. Lee teaches that only the overcomers in the
church belong to the Kingdom of heaven. This leads us
to the two stages of the Kingdom of heaven. The first
stage, its outward appearance and reality, coincides with
the period of the church, while the second stage, the
realization of the Kingdom of heaven, coincides with the
millennium.

---

[17]Witness Lee, "Entering the Kingdom of Heaven," *The Ministry
of the Word*, XLIII–LII (March–December, 1955), p. 819.

By the outward appearance of the Kingdom of heaven Lee means all Christendom, including both true and false Christians. The real Kingdom of heaven consists only of overcomers. One may be a Christian and yet not an overcomer. Thus in this age only those Christians who are overcomers live in the reality of the Kingdom of heaven. These believers who have paid a price, sought the anointing of the Spirit, been alert and prepared, will be raptured first and taken to the marriage supper. The unprepared believers will also be raptured, on a later day, but will not have the privilege of joining the marriage supper of the Lamb. They will also be reprimanded by the Lord.

During the millennial rule the Kingdom of heaven becomes realized. The overcomers will rule with Christ in heaven while the Jews and unprepared Christians will live on earth. After the thousand years, Christ will return the Kingdom to God and the Kingdom of heaven will officially cease to exist. The diagram on the following page explains the difference between the Kingdom of heaven and the Kingdom of God, and their development.

Lee believes that the outward appearance of the Kingdom of heaven is taught by the parable of the wheat and tares, the parable of the mustard seed, and the parable of the leaven (Matthew 13). In the first parable the wheat depicts true Christians while the tares are false Christians. In the second parable, we must recognize that normally the mustard seed would grow into a plant of vegetable size; but here it attains to the size of a tree, suggesting that the large number of false believers would make the Christian church look like a big organization and enable Satan (the birds of the air) to rest on it. In the last parable the woman is the Roman Catholic Church which has mixed into the pure teaching of the church different types of heresy and thus corrupted God's church, giving it a large outward appearance.

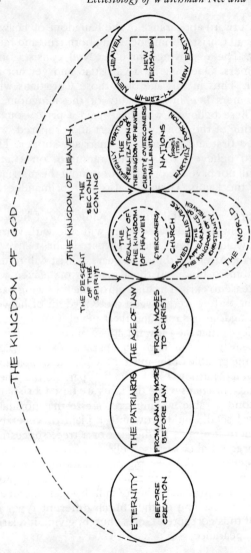

Where does the Bible teach the presently realized Kingdom of heaven? Lee finds it in the Sermon on the Mount.[18] In the Beatitudes Christ says that the Kingdom of heaven belongs to the poor in spirit and those who are persecuted. He here describes the spiritual condition of the overcomers. The kind of life exhibited by those who live under the rule of the heavens is also described in the other parts of the sermon. They are the salt and the light of the world (Matthew 5:13–16). Although they do not live under the Law, yet they live by a code of ethics which surpasses the Law (Matthew 5:17–48). They also suppress the activity of the flesh and are under the full control of the Spirit in their deeds of righteousness (Matthew 6:1–18). Their attitude toward material things of this world is described in Matthew 6:19–34. They are people who are able to love others as themselves (Matthew 7:1–11). Finally, all these righteous deeds are based on the principle of self-denial, which is described as the strait gate and the narrow way (Matthew 7:13–29).

The teaching of the future realization of the Kingdom of heaven, in the millennial age during which the overcomers rule in heaven with Christ, is based, according to Lee, on four important passages of Scripture. They are: Matthew 25:21–23; Matthew 19:28; Revelation 2:26,27; Revelation 20:4–6. Other passages that describe the same are Matthew 20:21–23; Matthew 24:46,47; Luke 19:17–19; II Timothy 2:12; and Revelation 3:21.

Lee is very careful in making a special doctrine out of this matter of entering the Kingdom of heaven. One may be a born-again Christian and yet not be able to enter the Kingdom of heaven in the millennial age. To enter the Kingdom of heaven is different from possessing eternal life. In Ephesians 2:8 and II Timothy 1:9 it is stated that we are saved by grace. There is, however, no

[18]*Ibid.,* pp. 807–815.

mention of grace, but only a crown of righteousness in
the matter of entering the Kingdom of heaven (II Timothy
4:8). This means that to enter the Kingdom of heaven,
deeds of righteousness are required. This difference is
also obvious when we compare Ephesians 2:8,9, which
says that salvation is not obtained by works, and Matthew
7:21, which declares that to enter the Kingdom of heaven
we need to do the will of God. Again, it is stated in
Romans 10:13 that those who call upon the name of
the Lord will be saved; yet in Matthew 7:21 our Lord
says, "Not everyone that saith unto me Lord, Lord, shall
enter into the kingdom of heaven." Finally, Paul says
in I Corinthians 5:1–5 that the man who committed fornication shall be saved, yet in I Corinthians 6:9,10 he says
that fornicators cannot inherit the Kingdom of God.
According to Lee, to inherit the Kingdom of God is to
enter the Kingdom of heaven.[19]

What are the blessings that those who manage to enter
the Kingdom of heaven will receive? Lee lists twelve kinds
from the Scriptures:

(1) They will rule with Christ for a thousand years
(Revelation 20:4, 6; II Timothy 2:12).

(2) They will receive crowns (II Timothy 4:8).

(3) They will sit on Christ's throne (Revelation 3:21).

(4) They will receive authority (Revelation 2:26,27;
Luke 19:17,19; Matthew 25:21,23).

(5) They will become priests (I Peter 2:9; Revelation
5:10; 1:6).

(6) They will inherit the land (Matthew 5:5).

(7) They will enter into the joy of the Lord (Matthew
25:21,23).

(8) They will enter the rest (Hebrews 4:1,11).

(9) They will be glorified together with Christ (Romans
8:17,18; I Peter 5:1).

[19]*Ibid.,* p. 858.

(10) They foretaste the blessings of the new Jerusalem (Revelation 2:7, 3:12).

(11) They will eat with the Lord at the marriage supper (Matthew 25:10; 26:29).

(12) They will eat the hidden manna (Revelation 2:17).[20]

There is, for Lee, ample Scriptural evidence for the punishment of unprepared Christians. He cites the following passages: Matthew 16:27; II Corinthians 5:10; Luke 14:33–35; Luke 12:45–48; Matthew 25:24–30; Matthew 24:48–51; John 15:5–6; I Corinthians 3:10–15; Matthew 10:24–33; Mark 8:38; Revelation 2:10,11 (not the second death as such here, but only the hurt of it); Revelation 3:4,5; Matthew 18:34,35; Matthew 5:22,29,30; Matthew 18:8,9; Mark 9:43–49; Hebrews 2:1–4; Hebrews 3:7—4:13; Hebrews 6:1–8; Hebrews 12:25–29.

For those who have become apprehensive and discouraged because of the high qualifications required to enter the Kingdom of heaven, there are assuring promises of the Lord in the Bible for those who sincerely seek. Luke 12:32 says, "Fear not, little flock; for it is your Father's good pleasure to give you the kingdom." It is also promised by God that for those who seek first His Kingdom and His righteousness, all these things, including the Kingdom and the righteousness, will be added to them (Matthew 6:33). Moreover our Lord has promised to meet those who seek, ask, and knock (Matthew 7:7). He also said, "If ye then, being evil, know how to give good gifts unto your children, how much more shall your Father which is in heaven give good things to them that ask him?" (Matthew 7:11). Not only is He willing to let us enter the Kingdom of heaven, He will also grant us strength to accomplish it. After telling His disciples how hard it is for a rich man to enter the Kingdom of heaven,

[20]*Ibid.,* pp. 908–915.

He, seeing that the disciples were discouraged, adds, "With men this is impossible; but with God all things are possible" (Matthew 19:26). Does not Paul tell us that Christ who is in us is mighty (II Corinthians 13:3)? He also reminds us that we "can do all things through Christ which strengtheneth [us]" (Philippians 4:13).

Of fundamental importance in Lee's doctrine of entering the Kingdom of heaven is the separation of true believers into two classes, the overcomers and the unprepared Christians. The former will be raptured before the tribulation and the latter after the tribulation. The overcomers will also rule over the other believers in the millennial Kingdom, which is made up of a heavenly portion where we have the ruling body of overcomers headed by Christ, and an earthly portion consisting of Jews, saved Christians of the New Testament epoch, and the other people of the world.[21]

In summary: The church, in Lee's theory, is part of the Kingdom of God. It had the same beginning, of course, as the Kingdom of heaven, which is also part of the Kingdom of God. The church is further divided into two classes of believers, those who are merely saved and those who overcome. Only the latter enter the Kingdom of heaven. So far as we have been able to determine, Watchman Nee, however, does not teach this.

The Essential Nature of the Church

Witness Lee has pointed out to us that the church is not a building; neither is it a denomination, a mission society, or any other organization. What then is the essen-

---

[21]Sound and scriptural as the reasoning by Lee in the preceding section may seem to be, it does have a basic weakness. We will discuss this at length in Chapter 5.

tial nature of the church? Both Nee and Lee recognize it as a living organism made up of believers called out of this world to gather together for fellowship, as the Greek word *ekklesia* indicates.

In their discussion of the nature of the church both Nee and Lee go to the Epistle to the Ephesians.[22] Nee divides it into six sections, each comprising one chapter. Chapter one deals with the Lord of the Body; chapter two, the material of the house; chapter three, the eternal mystery of the church; chapter four, the growth of the Body; chapter five, the preciousness of the Bride; and chapter six, the warfare of the people of God.

What does Paul mean by saying that the church is the Body of Christ? Neither Nee nor Lee understands it as simply a figure or symbol. The church is Christ![23] The last verse of the first chapter in Ephesians speaks of the church as the "fulness of Christ." The body is an expression of man's fullness. Likewise the church contains and expresses the fullness of Christ.

The second meaning of this Body is that it came out of Christ. This is treated in Ephesians 5:30–32. As Eve came out of Adam, so did the church come out of Christ. We have already noted Lee's theory of this unredemptive death of Christ.[24] Nee has the following to say on this aspect of the subject:

> Moreover the figure of the Church that Eve presents is a double figure, and this may help us to understand Paul's language in Ephesians. First, as a part of Adam, taken from him in sleep, she was his body. Then, created, perfected and brought again to him, she became his bride. Other created things were brought to him, but not being *of* him they could not be his help-meet. This distinguishes Eve from the rest

[22]Lee, *Understanding the Church*, pp. 3–16; Nee, *What Shall This Man Do?*, pp. 81–93.

[23]Nee, *loc. cit.*, p. 92.

[24]See p. 48

of the creation. It also typically distinguishes the Church of
Christ from the entire old creation today.[25]

Lee carries his typological explanation of the Biblical
figure one step further than Nee by saying that this organism is an actual Body of Christ, made up by putting
together the small portions of Christ we receive at our
salvation. Lee puts it in these words:

> The church is the Christ in you and in me. Putting together
> the portion of Christ in you, the portion of Christ in me,
> the portion of Christ in him, and those of all other Christians,
> we have the church.[26]

In Ephesians there is a mysterious section relating to
the church, wherein it is said that the church is both
the Bride and the Body (Ephesians 5:25–30). In verses
25–27 we have the first law of love in the command,
"Husbands, love your wives," noticing that it concerns
the past, speaking of Christ's redemptive love on Calvary.
There is also an implied future purpose of God for the
church. This speaks of the church as an eternal heavenly
entity. In verses 28–30 he calls attention to the present
aspect, that husbands ought also to love their own wives
as their own bodies. This speaks of Christ's love for His
church today. Nee sums up his view in these words:

> The first passage sees Christ and His Church apart, having
> separate existence, and is concerned with her union, as Bride,
> with Him, the Giver of life. The second sees Christ and
> His Church spiritually identified, without separate existence,
> and concerns her identification and present unity of life with
> Him as His Body. From one there have become two; from
> being two they will again be one. This is the mystery of
> the Church, that all that is from Christ returns to Him.[27]

---

[25]Nee, *loc. cit.*, p. 90.   [26]Lee, *loc. cit.*, p. 8.
[27]Nee, *loc. cit.*, pp. 91, 92.

This explains the united yet separate relationship between the church and her Christ in the expressions of the Body and the Bride. How does this unity come about? This is explained by the fact that the church is an extension of Christ, and thus is Christ. "Oh, brothers and sisters, the Church on earth today is Christ Himself. What a serious matter this is!" exclaims Lee.[28] Nee also states emphatically, ". . . because, speaking reverently, the Church *is* Christ!"[29] The Holy Spirit is instrumental in bringing about this union, as revealed in I Corinthians 12:13 wherein it is stated that we are all baptized into one body by the Holy Spirit.

The Bible also speaks of the church as the house of God. Ephesians 2:22 says, "In whom ye also are builded together for an habitation of God through the Spirit." Thus in the church God finds a resting place. Wherever God can live comfortably, there is His church. On the other hand, where God cannot feel at home, there we have only a religious organization.[30] A home is also the place where we best reveal our true identity and personality. In like manner, the church is a home wherein God can express and manifest Himself fully.

From what we have discussed, it is obvious that Nee and Lee view the church as not only a symbolic Body of Christ or an "extension" of Christ. It is, in the most literal sense of the word, the Body of Christ. However, it should be pointed out that they do not mean that the church is the continuation of the incarnation, as the Roman Catholics believe. All the members of the church have Christ in them. They live for Christ and carry on the work of Christ. It is in this sense that they can be called the Body of Christ.

---

[28]Lee, *loc. cit.,* p. 10.
[29]Nee, *loc. cit.,* p. 92.
[30]Lee, *loc. cit.,* p. 15.

The Unity of the Church

The Chinese characters for unity literally mean "to combine into one." Thus in speaking of the unity of the church, Witness Lee in one place shuns the use of this Chinese term.[31] Instead he calls it the "one origin" of the church. Both Nee and Lee believe that the church was one in unity to begin with. It is only when things are in a separate state that they can be combined into one. Lee has this to say in regard to this one origin of the church:

> The church comes from the triune God and thus has one source. The church is begun by the life of the triune God coming into us to become our life; and so the church has one beginning. The nature of the church is the life of the triune God becoming our life; therefore its nature is also one, because the principle produced by this nature must also be one. Moreover, the form of government everywhere is also one. The fellowship of the church in the entire universe is also one. Her testimony is one; and so are many other things. Therefore the church is one origin. There are seven ones in Ephesians 4:3–6; one body, one spirit, one hope, one Lord, one faith, one baptism, and one God. They all speak of the one origin of the church.[32]

This unity of the church should be the condition both of the church universal and of the local church. We shall have more to say about Nee's and Lee's concept of the local church. In this connection it is sufficient to point out that they believe that there should be only one church in any one locality. Denominationalism and sectarianism have disrupted this unity of the church on earth. Nee points out that in the very beginning, in the book of Acts, all the converts were called the church.[33] This gives him the insight that wherever a group of believers come together they automatically become a church regardless

[31]*Ibid.*, pp. 37–53.   [32]*Ibid.*, p. 38.
[33]Nee, *Rethinking Our Missions,* pp. 151-153.

of whether they have organization or constitution. It is also true that when a person comes to Christ at a certain place he automatically becomes a member of the church of that locality. If we require him to have something else before accepting him into the church, then ours is not a church but a denomination; and thus the unity of the church is destroyed.

Nee also points out that the unity of the church is not something man-made.[34] This unity is given to every Christian the moment he becomes a Christian. It is a common possession of all true Christians. Note that Paul exhorts all the Christians in Ephesus to *keep* the unity of the Spirit, which they already have, not to *produce* unity.

Believers were all one to start with, at both the universal and local levels. How was this unity ruined, and what are the remedies suggested? In his book *The Way of the Church,* Watchman Nee points out the three methods being followed by different groups in Christendom in their efforts to bring about unity.

The first one is the Roman Catholic way to unity. In the apostolic age there were individual churches, and the apostles did not combine them into one united organization. But after the apostles, changes came gradually in the form of the church. The churches in the cities became large and powerful. Rural churches were amalgamated to become their satellite churches. This called for changes in church administration and government. Some held that the authority of the apostles was passed on to the elders. One elder was chosen from the city church to become the bishop, who superintended the city church and all the satellite rural churches. This trend of concentration continued throughout the Roman Empire until the Bishop of Rome became the head of all the other bishops. He

---

[34]*Ibid.*, p. 157.

was called the Pope. From that time on the "churches" of the Bible became the one Catholic Church. Not understanding fully the Scriptural teaching on the nature of the church, no one dared attack the vices within the Catholic Church. Believing that there was only one church in the world, no one dared protest against the false teachings of the Roman Church or leave it.[35] Thus, for over a thousand years, effort was made to keep this unity of the church. Even when Luther came on the scene, his original intention was to reform and not to split—though he was eventually forced to do so. This kind of organizational unity of the church, according to Nee, is most unbiblical. In the Bible he sees only independent local churches. Thus there were churches in the province of Judea and also churches in the province of Galatia; there was no such a thing as joining all these churches into one organized church. It is therefore clear that this Roman Catholic way to unity is unscriptural.

The second way to unity, according to Nee, is called spiritual unity. It is practiced by the state churches and denominations.

When Martin Luther started the Reformation there were states in Europe whose rulers had already become apprehensive of the Pope's growing influence in secular affairs. Seeking for a way to rid themselves of the grip of the Roman Church, these princes found a ready instrument in Martin Luther and other leaders of the Reformation. This accounts for the rise of national churches in Europe, and especially so in the case of England. What happened to these states was that everyone born in a particular state automatically became a member of the

[35]It appears that Nee's purpose at this point was better served by not making reference to the separation in 1054 of the Catholic Church into Eastern Orthodoxy and Roman Catholicism, this being in no sense a spiritual reformation. He also overlooks the Waldenses of the twelfth century and the Hussites of the fourteenth.

state church. But later an awkward situation arose because many did not believe in the teaching of their own church. They were members of the state church, yet they were not Christians. This embarrassing situation called for the emergence of the doctrine of "the visible and invisible church." According to this doctrine, in the visible institutional church there are both believers and non-believers. The Christians in the invisible church are all spiritual believers, and thus have a spiritual unity even though the visible church does not have this unity.

Those who advocate this teaching regarding the visible and invisible churches often cite the parable of the wheat and the tares for support of the doctrine—the wheat being the true Christians while the tares are the false Christians. Yet they forget that our Lord says that the field is the world and not the church. On the other hand, it is certainly true that what they regard as the visible church is actually the world which they have made into a church. But the church, as we have seen, is Scripturally made up only of believers called out of the world.

The book of Revelation refers to the churches as lampstands. What is a lampstand? It is the place from which light shines forth. Jesus says that our light should shine before men and that we should not put our light under a bushel. Thus it is ridiculous and impossible to have an invisible church, for the church would be an invisible light.[36]

Not only did the state churches advocate a spiritual unity, denominational churches also believe in it. How did denominations come about? They arose because there were dissenters who did not agree with some of the teachings of their state churches. So in the name of defending certain doctrines, men left the large state churches to form the Baptist Church, the Mennonite Church, the

[36] Nee, *The Way of the Church,* p. 65.

Society of Friends, etc. In the beginning there were serious disputes, but after a few generations the disputants began to cool down and soon came to think that they should shake hands with each other. This accounts for the united activities among most denominations today. This, to Nee, is like holding hands over the fence. For him, this does not solve the problem. It is also hypocrisy. For if it is wrong to build up denominational walls, then they must be pulled down completely. Otherwise this interdenominational kind of unity is no unity at all, according to Nee.

The third way to unity is that advocated by the Baptists and the Congregationalists. They believe in the independent church. It is different from the local church principle, however, in that it allows for more than one independent church in one locality. Thus they have come very close to the Biblical principle of independent local churches, yet they have overstepped and gone wrong. The kind of unity they stress is the fellowship and cooperation practiced among independent congregations.

What Nee sees wrong with this kind of system is that it violates the Scriptural principle of "one locality, one church." It also makes it easy for a minority group in the church to pull out and start a new church when they have different opinions. Moreover, it is unscriptural and is condemned by Paul in I Corinthians. When some Christians say "I belong to Paul," there emerges a Pauline independent congregation. When some say "I belong to Apollos," there comes forth an Apollos independent congregation. According to Nee, this is the activity of the flesh, which cannot produce real unity.

Thus we have local churches in the apostolic age. Later they were combined to become provincial and district churches. Finally they were united to become one international church. Eventually there was the schism between the Eastern and Western churches. Then there emerged the Reformation which broke up the one large international Western church. Yet it did not dissolve into the original type of local churches. It was broken up into national churches. Later these national churches were further dissolved into denominations and independent churches. These came closer and closer to the true Scriptural principle of unity at every step. But it was only when the Brethren Movement arose in the nineteenth century that the original principle of the local church and unity was restored. Unfortunately, the Brethren later were split up into two separate groups. One followed a united church principle and the other followed the independent church principle.

True Biblical unity, Nee points out, is the unity of the Body. Scripture teaches that the church is the Body of Christ. It is only reasonable and obvious that this Body, wherein lives the one Spirit, cannot be divided. How is this unity displayed? It is not exhibited by forming one large catholic church on earth, as the Roman Catholics might like to think. This one institutional church is not taught by Scripture. If it is God's purpose to have one church on earth, then the word "churches" should not appear in the Bible. In the book of Revelation we are told that for every church on earth there is one golden lampstand in heaven. In the Old Testament there was one lampstand with seven branches, representing the united nation of Israel. It is not so in the New Testament. We see that there are seven separate lampstands with Christ walking among them. If it is one lampstand with seven branches, then Christ would not be able to walk among them. Is it not obvious, asks Nee, that the unity of the church does not mean one united church on earth?

On the other hand, to practice denominationalism and at the same time promote spiritual unity is also unscriptural. What then is God's will for the display of this unity on earth?

There are two books in the New Testament which contain special revelations concerning the church: Ephesians and Colossians. The church referred to in these two epistles is one made up of all the Christians all over the world in the past, at the present, and also in the future. This is the church universal. There is a real spiritual unity in this church. If we speak of only this kind of unity, however, then it is easy for us to slip into denominationalism and be promoting a spiritual unity which is only a theory. Fortunately God gives us three other books in the New Testament which deal with another kind of unity. These are the Corinthian epistles and the letter to the Philippians, which speak also of the unity of the Body. Yet this is not the unity of the universal church but that of the local church, for what Paul is dealing with is disagreements and schism in one local church. He is exhorting the believers in Corinth and Philippi to "keep the unity." Thus it should be clear to us that God's will is for the unity of the church to be displayed and manifested in the local church. This does not mean, on the other hand, that there should be no fellowship between local churches. Yes, there *should be* spiritual communication between local churches, Nee stresses, but not between differing denominations in one locality, for these should not be. The Biblical principle is "one church at one locality." Nee thus concludes that spiritual unity is between local churches and not among denominations.

So of the four schools of thought regarding unity, as Nee analyzes matters, the only proper one, naturally, is what he understands to be the Biblical one. It demands that all within the denominations leave these unscriptural organizations and join local churches. If they do that, all in one locality will become one church, and thus unity is preserved. Denominationalism is therefore the greatest hindrance to church unity. Both Nee and Lee condemn denominations and the schismatic nature of the Protestant church in very strong words. Lee in great indignation has this to say about the Protestant segment of Christendom:

> It is out and out the church of Jesus Christ. Why do they put up the sign: "Wesleyan," or "Luther." Don't think this is a trivial matter. If this is not spiritual fornication, what is it? One church with scores of names affixed to it. How is it different from a woman who bears the names of scores of husbands?[37]

Thus, for Lee, the Protestant church is as much a spiritual harlot as the Roman Catholic Church.

What are the causes for this great disunity in today's church? How did denominations come about? Lee gives six major causes for this heart-breaking schismatic condition.[38] The first is the use of special names. The only name that should be given to a church is the name of the city it is in. Thus we have "the church in Corinth" and "the church in Antioch." But today in the Protestant church, some use the name of a person, like Luther or Wesley, to name their churches. Some use the special doctrine that they emphasize, such as the Hsin-I Church (信義會) which in English means "Justification by Faith Church," or Sheng-Chieh Church (聖潔會) which means "Holiness Church." Some use names of different systems of church government as names, such as the Presbyterian Church or the Episcopalian Church. The Anglican Church and the Church of China use the names of their nations as the names of their churches. The Baptists and others name their churches after the rites they stress. But whenever we add other names to the church of God, we become denominations.

The second cause is the emphasis on particular doctrines. There should be no other doctrines for special

[37]Lee, *Understanding the Church.* p. 44.   [38]*Ibid.*

emphasis besides the seven "one's" in Ephesians 4. But today there are groups of Christians who go beyond these. One of the doctrines of the Anglican creed is: "I believe in the Anglican Church."[39] The Seventh-Day Adventists believe so strongly in the keeping of the Sabbath that they will not accept as members those who do not believe in the seventh-day Sabbath for Christians.

The third cause is the establishment of special fellowship. This happens when certain Baptists and some of the Brethren groups will not break bread with those who do not belong to their groups.

The fourth cause is the practice of isolation and the neglect of universal fellowship. This describes those who, realizing the error of denominationalism, leave the institutional churches and avoid all names and the emphasis of special doctrines. Yet they do not have fellowship with all those who believe and practice the same Biblical principles, and thus become "local denominations."

The fifth is having more than one governing body in one locality. There are those who have seen the light of the local church in the Bible and have left denominations. Yet they do not join the local group in existence, which is already functioning under sound Biblical principles of the local church. Although they have certain communication with the local church, they have their own elders and form their own church government. This again causes them to become denominations.

This last cause is a very subtle one. It is the situation in which a group appears to have no special title or doctrine. Everything seems right except that it has some connection with certain Christian organizations. It is this little attachment that disqualifies it from being a proper local church.

The above six causes of disunity are used by Lee to

---

[39]The accuracy of this assertion is questionable.

serve as criteria in determining whether a certain Christian group is a denomination or not.

At this point, one may begin to realize that Nee and Lee think every other Christian group has gone wrong, including even the Brethren groups. Yes, they do not recognize any other institutional churches or denominations as churches. They, with their emphasis on locality as the only Scriptural distinction and demarcation, are the only true church. Yet others might taunt them by pointing out that they, by separating themselves from others, are actually adding another denomination to the existing schismatic situation. They are conscious of this type of argument against them and are quite prepared to defend themselves against it. Lee has cited an incident in the past when he was defending his own group on this particular issue while he was in mainland China. This, in the present writer's opinion, constitutes the best self-defense given for their position. An important passage embodying the defense follows:

> In 1937 when I returned to Yuen-Tai from Tientsin, a brother invited me for supper. I'll never forget that incident. He had also invited some church leaders to that supper. While we were eating an elderly brother questioned me: "Mr. Lee, you have always said that there is only one church, which cannot be divided. Why then do you separate yourselves from us? When you do this isn't it true that you form another denomination? I am glad to have this opportunity tonight to hear what you have to say on this." I said, "Very good. I have been looking for such an opportunity to settle this matter with you." That elderly brother happily agreed, saying that it was good. "Let's have it straightened out between us," said he. Then I said, "First of all, we know that Paul in his days condemned those Corinthians who claimed to belong to Paul, Apollos, or Peter. Obviously they were wrong when they did that. Now let me ask you: Is it wrong for us today to claim that we belong to the Church of China, to the Baptist Church, or to the Presbyterian Church?" They

answered, "No doubt that is wrong." "Very well," I said, "the first point is clear. My second question is: Which church do you want me to belong to: the Presbyterian Church, the Baptist Church, the Church of China, or one of the other churches?" They said, "We don't want you to belong to the Presbyterian Church, or the Baptist Church, or the Church of China, or any other church." I said, "Then this point is also clear. The third question is: Can I, one who has received mercy and much blessing from the Lord, shun the responsibility of preaching the gospel?" They answered, "Of course you have to preach the gospel." I pursued with another question, "Where am I supposed to send all my converts? Could I send them to the denominational churches when I do not go there myself?" "Surely you cannot, since you don't go yourself," they said. Again I said, "What should I do then? Do I need to hold services for them after they are saved?" They said, "Surely, they need to have meetings." I said, "Well, since they need to meet, where could they meet? If I go to meeting with them in the Baptist Church, then I am guilty of division with the Presbyterian Church. If I go to the Church of China with them, then I also create a division with the Presbyterians. Please tell me where I should go with them for fellowship?" At this point they could argue with me no more and had to keep quiet. Then I continued, "My friends you must realize that we meet at the Fourth Avenue because we are forced out of the church by you. How much we wish that all the children of God could be united. However, we have been pressed by you to leave, and so have to go humbly to meet at the Fourth Avenue. So we did not separate ourselves from you, but you separate yourselves from us. The responsibility for division is on you and not on us. You have forced us into such a situation. Now I would like to ask you to do one thing for me. You are all representatives of your denominations. You go and cancel all the titles like the Presbyterian Church, the Church of China, China Inland Mission, and so on, then I will go and close down our service at the Fourth Avenue. So we will not be divided anymore." When they heard such a demand, they were shocked and said, "How can we do that!" I said, "If you are not able to do such a thing, then you have nothing to say. Your division is so deep-rooted that there is actually no way out. We must go to meet at a place which does not belong to any denomination. And yet you say we ourselves made the division. Please tell me who is responsible for this division?"[40]

The Gifts of God to the Church

There are four important lists of the gifts of God in the New Testament. In Ephesians 4:11 there are mentioned: apostles, prophets, evangelists, pastors and teachers. In the list in Romans 12:6–8 there are: prophecy, ministry, teaching, exhortation, ruling, and showing mercy. In I Corinthians 12:8–10, the list is made up of: the word of wisdom, the word of knowledge, faith, healing, working of miracles, prophecy, discerning of spirits, tongues, interpretation of tongues. The list in I Corinthians 12:28 consists of: apostles, prophets, teachers, miracles, gifts of healings, helps, governments, diversities of tongues.

According to Nee, the four gifts in Ephesians are gifts of God to the church.[41] The gifts in I Corinthians 12:8–10 he calls miraculous gifts, which are given to individual Christians. Those in Romans 12 are also gifts for the individual, except that they are ordinary gifts of grace obtained when we become believers. The nine in I Corinthians 12:8–10 are given when believers are under the special power of the Holy Spirit. On the other hand, those in Romans 12 are for believers so that they may function effectively as members of the Body. I Corinthians 12 lays emphasis on power while Romans 12 stresses life. Those listed in I Corinthians 12:28 are gifts to the church, while those mentioned earlier in the chapter are gifts to individuals. Another distinction which Nee makes

[40]Lee, *loc. cit.* pp. 78–86.
[41]Nee, *The Normal Christian Church Life.* pp. 17–22.

is that the first list in the chapter is of gifts for the local church, while the second list is of gifts for the church universal. From these eight mentioned in I Corinthians 12:28, God has chosen the four mentioned in Ephesians to achieve His specific goal in the church.

The four gifts to the church listed in Ephesians are men—men who have received personal gifts as mentioned in I Corinthians 12 and Romans 12. They are a very special type of person, sent by God to the church for its upbuilding. Theirs are not ministries given to every Christian, but only to those called to that special ministry for the church.

Nee also brings to our attention that pastors and teachers are one gift, not two. The first three are each mentioned with a prefix "some," while only one "some" is used for "pastors and teachers." This is a strong indication that there are only four classes of persons that Paul had in mind. Actually the two kinds of ministries are so closely connected that, for all practical purposes, they should be considered as one. Those who teach must also shepherd and those who shepherd must also be able to teach.

Teaching is a gift of grace (for it appears in Romans 12) and not a miraculous gift, and that is why it is omitted in the list of miraculous gifts in I Corinthians 12:8–10. Thus teachers are, in Nee's own words, "individuals who have received the gift of teaching from Christ and have been given by the Lord to His Church for its upbuilding." It should also be noticed that they concern themselves mainly with interpretation and not revelation, which is the work of the prophets.

Evangelists are also gifts to the church. (There is, however, no such a thing as an "evangelistic gift" in the Bible.) There are only two other occasions where the noun "evangelist" is used: Philip is referred to in Acts 21:8 as an evangelist; Paul in II Timothy 4:5 encouraged Timothy to do the work of an evangelist. However, the verb derived from the same root occurs quite often. Nee confesses that he is not exactly sure of the sphere of work of the evangelist. But the fact that the Holy Spirit did not descend upon Philip's converts when he preached in Samaria seems to indicate, says Nee, that evangelists are supposed to confine their work to one place, while the apostle is to work in many places.

The gift of prophecy is mentioned in all four lists, indicating that it is both a personal gift and a gift to the church. It is a miraculous gift as well as a gift of grace. Prophecy is an office for the universal church and the prophet is also a man given by God for the special ministry.

The apostles differ from the other three classes of God's servants in that theirs is an office and not a gift. They might have personal gifts of prophecy and teaching, but what constitutes them apostles is their commission and not their gifts. We shall discuss more about Nee's view on the office of the apostle when we come to the matter of church government. It suffices to mention here that Nee regards apostles as men commissioned by God to evangelize and start local churches in all places. It is also important to note that Nee does not advocate the perpetuation of the special office of the twelve apostles of our Lord. He has this to say concerning the difference between the twelve apostles and the other apostles:

> The Lord Jesus has now gone, but the Spirit has come.
> . . . The Son came to accomplish the will of the Father;
> the Spirit has come to accomplish the will of the
> Son. . . . The Son while on earth appointed "the twelve"
> to be apostles. The Son has returned to the Father, and now
> the Spirit is on earth appointing other men to be apostles.
> The apostles appointed by the Holy Spirit cannot join the
> ranks of those appointed by the Son, but nonetheless they
> are apostles. . . . We must differentiate clearly between the
> apostles who were witnesses to the resurrection of Christ

(Acts 1:22,26) and the apostles who are ministers for the edifying of the Body of Christ. It is evident, therefore, that God has *other* apostles besides the original twelve.[42]

The Mission of the Church to the World

In all Nee's writings the present writer has not come across any direct discussion of the great commission of Matthew 28. This does not mean, however, that he does not believe in the evangelization of the whole world or that missionary work is not his concern. As a matter of fact, he believes missionary work to be the most important duty of the church. The training and upbuilding of Christians is, naturally, the major activity of the church; yet for him this is not the primary duty of the church. He says:

> No doubt, the church on earth needs feeding. I believe in feeding. I also believe that in China there is nobody else that believes in feeding the way I do. But I have to admit, the commission of the church on earth is not to feed, but to preach the gospel.[43]

Because China was largely unevangelized it was Nee's conviction and primary concern to evangelize the whole of China. Churches in some other lands might properly major in feeding, but the situation in China was not the same. So the church in China, he felt, must give priority to evangelization and missionary work. He recalls one conversation with a Mr. Sparks in which he expresses this great need in China:

> When I was in London I told Mr. Sparks that our work in China is different from theirs. We have to preach the gospel.

[42]*Ibid.*, pp. 14, 15.
[43]Watchman Nee, *The Business of the Church* (Taiwan: Gospel Book Room, 1968), p. 77.

They have so many Christians in London and vicinity that it is just like a Christian nation. We are not in the same situation. We must preach the gospel the same way they did in the beginning. What our brothers in London are doing is just one kind of ministry. But we must preach the gospel.[44]

For Nee, their mission field is not the world but China, a vast land with a huge population. Surely there was enough work for them in China. How is it possible for the whole of China to be reached by the gospel? It must be done by the total mobilization of the entire church in the work. Every believer must be an evangelist or a missionary. It must be the work of all and not the few or even the many in the church. All New Testament saints are priests and so all must serve. In Nee's own words:

> The concept before was that there must be many who do the work. Today we must make a change. The *entire* church must work. . . . If the church does not grow to a stage when the entire church works and serves, it is no church. When the whole church rises up to work and to serve, immediately we see the Body of Christ.[45]

For the purpose of preaching the gospel and giving all believers the opportunity to get involved and to serve, Nee advocates the abolition of the traditional Sunday worship service. Instead, the time should be employed for evangelistic work in which all believers take part. We shall have more to say on this when we come to the discussion on church meetings.[46]

How can the church fulfill the great missionary commission of the Lord? Nee suggests two fundamental Biblical methods. The one he calls the Antioch way and the other he calls the Jerusalem way.[47] The first way is the sending

---

[44]Nee, *Rethinking Our Missions.* p. 343.
[45]Nee, *The Business of the Church.* p. 79.
[46]See p. 119.   [47]Nee, *Rethinking Our Missions.* p. 341.

out of apostles to plant churches all over the country. After founding and establishing a church, the apostle then appoints elders to take charge of that local church and moves on to another place. This was what Paul, Barnabas, Timothy, and Silas did. (The office and work of the apostle as seen by Nee will be treated in detail when we discuss church affairs.)

A more important and effective way is the second way, the emigration method. This involves the moving out of a Christian family to settle in a place where no Christian witness exists, for the purpose of evangelizing that place. According to Nee, whether we go in peace or because of persecution is not an important matter. The pattern and example is there in the Bible for us to follow.

After making converts the church should immediately give them basic training in Christian living and service. The training devised by Watchman Nee is a course of fifty-two lessons designed for one year. After the training is over, the converts are to be sent out as emigrants to places where the gospel is needed.

One may wonder how when Nee and his followers put this plan into operation they managed to supply proper leadership and qualified elders to direct the local churches that had just come into existence. This they solved by having these new churches send good men to a place called Kuling to receive proper training. Believing very strongly in this kind of evangelistic emigration work, Nee was confident of reaching all of China with the gospel in a short time. His vision he states in this way:

> This [the missionary method of emigration] means the whole church is engaged in preaching the gospel, and not only a few evangelists doing the work. If the work is done only by the evangelists, there won't be much accomplishment in a whole lifetime's preaching. Today we have four hundred and fifty million people in China with only a million Christians. The only hope is to put the million believers in our hand

and send them all out. Give them the same kind of training, send them out, then you see the entire church preaching the gospel.[48]

The Purposes of God for the Church

Many have seen the church merely as an instrument in God's hands for the winning of souls. This is certainly one of God's purposes for the church. But there are other functions of the church that God has designated it to fulfill. "The highest purpose God has for the Church today," Nee says, "is that she should build herself up in love by a ministry of life, and so grow up in all things into Christ."[49] Both Nee and Lee emphasize very strongly the church's ministry of evangelism. Yet it is the building up and mutual edification that is the more important ministry that God has purposed the church to do.

Nee tells us that the Bible speaks of two "Christs," the personal Christ and the corporate Christ.[50] The personal Christ has already won complete victory, but the corporate Christ, which is the church plus the personal Christ, has not yet attained this victory in actual experience. In terms of the true knowledge of Christ and faith, the church is still a babe. God's purpose is for the church to grow up into the full stature of Christ. This is accomplished through mutual edification of the members.

It is when the church grows up to the fullness of Christ (Ephesians 1:23) that the moral glory of Christ can be manifested.[51] When this happens, God's purpose for the

[48]Ibid., p. 348.
[49]Nee, What Shall This Man Do?, p. 111. At this point, let us notice that at another place we have quoted Nee as saying that the more important ministry of the church is evangelism and not edification. See p. 80.
[50]Nee, Rethinking Our Missions, pp. 29, 30.
[51]Lee, The Ministry of the Word, LVII-LXL, p. 1047.

church is realized. Adam needed Eve for his fullness; so in the same way Christ needs the church for His fullness. Christ needed a body to manifest the glory of the Godhead in Palestine almost two thousand years ago; today the church is serving the very function that His body did while He was on earth. With regard to this, Witness Lee has these important words to say:

> But Christ has also a Body in the universe. This Body is the church of the ages. Christ, who has ascended to heaven, is still living on this earth through this Body. Through this Body He has extended Himself through the centuries, and has also expanded Himself over the entire world. . . . In the four Gospels He allows us to see Him living through Jesus of Nazareth, in Acts He lets us see Himself living through the Church. As a matter of fact it is not the Acts of the Apostles. It should be called the Acts of Christ continued. . . . Therefore the first function of the church in the universe is to succeed Christ, extend Christ and expand Christ, that is to say, to be the fullness of Christ in time and space in the universe, in order that the whole universe recognize this fullness. It requires all the believers all over the world in all ages to demonstrate this fullness.[52]

Another purpose God has for the church is to become His temple and household (Ephesians 2:21,22). God's original abode is in heaven. But in order to manifest His glory and to do His will here on earth, God must have a household on earth.

God's purpose is also for the church to demonstrate to Satan and his followers the manifold wisdom of God even now (Ephesians 3:10). God's adversary might have thought that he had frustrated or even ruined God's purpose for creation. But God is one who knows no defeat. He was able to establish His Kingdom through the redemptive work of Christ. This church, created through the redemptive work of Christ, manifests God's wisdom,

[52]*Ibid.,* p. 1048.

and is also the means by which Satan was defeated.

On the practical level, these purposes of God can be accomplished by the three kinds of ministries: evangelism, building up of believers, and service. The way to make Christ manifested is by winning souls from the clutch of Satan and giving them the life of Christ. After one becomes a Christian the next important step is to train him to lead a God-centered, victorious Christian life. Finally, a person not only needs to be saved and receive training, but he also has to be led into service. Only by doing these things well can we build up God's church and manifest the glory of Christ.[53]

The Destiny of the Church

God today is preparing the church to become the Bride. Unfortunately the church today, as Nee sees it, is a "leaking vessel," unable to contain what the Head has to give.[54] There are blemishes and imperfections in the Body. It is "by water with the word" that the church is being changed into the likeness of Christ, until at the Second Coming of our Lord the church will be presented to Him as a "glorious church, not having spot, or wrinkle, or any such thing" (Ephesians 5:27). As Nee puts it: "Wholly like Him because wholly of Him, she will be wholly for Him."[55] This is the time when God's purpose for the church becomes fully realized.

According to Lee, the Bride is also the New Jerusalem which John saw coming down from heaven.[56] All true believers belong to the New Jerusalem. There in that

[53]Witness Lee, *Government by Elders* (Taiwan: Gospel Book Room, 1968), p. 195.

[54]Nee, *What Shall This Man Do?*, p. 149.

[55]*Ibid.*, p. 93.

[56]Lee, *The Glorious Church*, p. 129.

city the curse of Genesis 3 shall be done away with
(Revelation 22:3). There is no more death. Sin belongs
to the history of the past. In short, what the Fall has
brought about will be abolished. All the glory that belongs
to the church will be recovered.[57] In that day the church
will also submit to the sovereign rule of God. The right
relationship between God and man will be established
forever. The same verse also tells us that all believers
will be God's servants, serving Him in eternity. Not only
will the church eternally serve God, there will also be
fellowship with Him. Believers will walk in the light of
God, as verse 5 indicates. The most important aspect
of the eternal destiny of the church is the eternal kingship
of all believers (Revelation 22:5). With this all of God's
original intention for man is materialized. This will be
the glorious state of the church as Lee sees it in the
Bible.

[57]*Ibid.*, p. 156.

Chapter 4

THE CHURCH LOCAL

The Nature of the Local Church

If there is any one doctrine which Nee and his associates stress with the greatest emphasis, and one which distinguishes them from all other Christian groups, it is their doctrine of the local church.

According to this doctrine, locality is the only Scriptural basis for the division of the church into churches. Nee defines localities as:

> Places of convenient size for people to live together in a certain measure of safety and sociability. In modern language we should call them cities. . . . Any place is qualified to be a unit for the founding of a church which is a place where people group together to live, a place with an independent name, and a place which is the smallest political unit.[1]

In large cities like London and New York there is more than one such locality because there are several administrative units, such as boroughs and postal districts. Each of these, then, is regarded as one unit-locality. On a smaller scale, country places like villages and towns are also regarded as separate units. Nee reminds us that Christ went into cities and villages to preach (Luke 13:22).

In the Bible, so Nee tells us, there are no names attached to the churches other than the names of the cities. This is the case with the seven churches in Asia referred to in the book of Revelation.

[1]Nee, *The Normal Christian Church Life*, p. 48.

The limits of the churches must not be narrower than a locality. It happened in the church of Corinth in Paul's days that her members attempted to split the local church into factions, the Paul sect, the Apollos sect, the Cephas sect, and the Christ sect. We also notice that in Jerusalem, although there were many believers, yet it was referred to as one church, the church of Jerusalem.

But what about churches in the house as mentioned in Romans 16:5, Colossians 4:15, and Philemon 2? Nee's answer to this is that the membership was small in the early days of these churches and so they could conveniently meet in a believer's house, and so the church in the house is identical with the church of that city.[2] The church in Priscilla and Aquila's house is therefore the church of Rome. Likewise later when the couple moved to Ephesus (Acts 18:2, 18, 19) they also led an assembly in their house (I Corinthians 16:19). Yet from Revelation 2:1 we infer that there is only one church in Ephesus. The church in Nymphas' house (Colossians 4:15) is the church in Laodicea, as we see in the next verse. Again, in Revelation 3:14, we discover that there is only one church in Laodicea. In Philemon 2 the church spoken of is actually the church of Colossae, as we can see from Colossians 1:2 and 4:17. The conclusion Nee draws is that all these churches in the houses are simply the churches of those particular cities.

On the other hand, Nee also sees in the Bible no churches larger than localities. There is no such a thing as "the church in Macedonia" or "the church in Judea," because these are provinces. There is only "the *churches* of a certain province or district" (I Corinthians 16:19; Galatians 1:2; II Corinthians 8:1, 18–24). There is therefore no Scriptural warrant for combining all the churches in one district into a synod.

---

[2]Lee, *The Ministry of the Word.* LVII–LXI, pp. 1067, 1068.

This leads us to the Scriptural teaching that all the local churches are independent in responsibilities and government. The authority of the local church is also absolutely final; there is no court of appeal higher than the local church.

This does not mean, however, that the local churches should have nothing to do with one another. They are still members of the one universal Body of believers. On a spiritual level there is interdependency because they have one life and one Lord. The Bible teaches that "the responsibility of the churches is individual, but their actions should be uniform."[3] In I Corinthians 4:17 we read that Paul sent Timothy to deliver to the Corinthian church certain teachings which he also taught the other churches. In I Corinthians 7:17 Paul asked the Corinthian church to obey the same command of the Lord as he had asked other churches to obey. The example of churches helping each other and learning from each other is seen in Paul's exhortation to the Corinthians in the matter of collecting offerings (I Corinthians 16:1). Paul also relates that the brothers in Thessalonica were "followers of the churches of God which in Judea are in Christ Jesus" (I Thessalonians 2:14).

Thus there is balance in the teaching of God about intra-church relationships. There is independence of local churches concerning matters of outward organization and government; but at the same time there is mutual edification and fellowship with one another spiritually.

How can this local character of the church be preserved? Nee suggests two ways. The first has to do with the attitude of the "apostle," Nee's word for church-planting missionary. He should always be concerned with planting and building a local church and not the setting up of a church of his liking or one that is under his control.

[3]Nee, *loc. cit.*, p. 52.

He should not attempt to gather people around him with the emphasis on certain doctrines or teachings. The second is the prevention of the linking up of local churches to form a federation.

Nee sees great advantages in this independent local church system. First of all, it prevents ambitious workers from planting churches and starting sects of their own. If there is only one church in one locality, there is no room for dissension which leads to denominationalism. In short, it is the only way to church unity.

He feels also that this plan serves as a deterrent to the spread of heresy. When a heresy arises in one local church the other churches may not be easily affected. But in a federal system like that of the Roman Catholic Church, heresy affects the entire organization everywhere.

One may wonder how this doctrine could be carried out on a practical level in face of the existing divided condition of Christendom. In the past, in their obedience to what they think is the Scriptural teaching concerning the nature of the local church, Nee and his associates have encountered much misunderstanding and criticism. It is to clear up these misconceptions that Lee has formulated an eighteen-point declaration of their practice and attitude.[4] The nine points in the declaration concerning practice are:

(1) We abandon all other bases for establishing a local church, and return to the basis of "one church at one locality."

(2) Having established our church according to this basis of "one church at one locality," we act according to the principle of the true local church. We assemble for meetings and coordinate to serve in such a manner as to live out what the Body of Christ ought to be, striving to manifest the life of Christ as a living witness. We desire to be built up to become God's household where God can manifest Himself

[4] Lee, *Understanding the Church,* pp. 99–125.

and have His will carried out.

(3) It is not our intention to found a unique sect, and to establish "our assembly" everywhere.

(4) We are willing to accept people with whatever kind of doctrines and views insofar as they do not contradict the fundamental elements of the gospel.

(5) Believing in the necessity for church unity, we are willing to fellowship and to serve the Lord with whatever Christian groups that have sound doctrines but different opinions if they are willing not to form a separate group.

(6) We accept all kinds of Christians holding to different doctrines, under the condition that they have not committed sins that make them liable to be excommunicated.

(7) We are willing to have fellowship with all brothers and sisters in all denominations, but we refuse to have anything to do with their denominational prejudices.

(8) Although we accept brothers and sisters who do not see things the way we see them, we cannot trust them with any responsibility in service.

(9) We encourage brothers and sisters, whenever they come to a new place, to join existing assemblies that hold to the true local church principle, and to attend their meetings and to serve with them. But if there are no such assemblies, then they should begin preaching the gospel and bring people to know Christ. At the same time they should lead those who are already Christians to know the true nature of the church, and to start a meeting on the true local church basis.

Witness Lee also formulates nine points to sum up their attitude:

(1) We are not the Roman Catholic Church or the Protestant Church. We recognize neither the Roman Church nor the Protestant Church.

(2) We are not a so-called Brethren group, either the Exclusive Brethren, or the Open Brethren.

(3) We are not those who have left the Roman Church or the Protestant Church and become formless little sects without a definite stand. We hold meetings according to definite church principles.

(4) We do not consider ourselves the whole of the local church in any place. We realize that we are only part of the local church, built on the basis of the local church principle.

(5) We recognize all saved ones in all groups including the Roman Church as our brothers and sisters in the Lord. But we would say that they have already lost the correct basis of the true local church.

(6) According to the revelation of the Bible we know that both the Roman Church and the Protestant Church will not change or cancel themselves, so we do not expect them to do so. All we wish is that people would leave them and return to the local church established on the right basis.

(7) We recognize all those kinds of church unities promoted by people who stand firm on denominational grounds as useless and not thorough. They do not do any good to the church's testimony. They divide and yet unite, unite and yet divide.

(8) Any work outside the church which is not conducive to the building up of the local church should not exist. We do not want to have anything to do with such people.

(9) Although this is our attitude, yet we realize that our God is a great God. He can use all kinds of people, even those who hold to unbiblical doctrines like those of the Roman Catholic Church.

The Government and Organization of the Church

In view of the strong emphasis Nee places on divine sovereignty and authority, it goes without saying that he has no argument with those who say that the government of the church, as regards the source of authority, is an absolute monarchy. Christ is the head of the church which is His Body. As to the interpretation and execution of the will of Christ, however, the entire authority is delegated to the elders. The elders are the authority of the church.[5] They represent and execute the authority

---

[5]Lee, *Government by Elders*. p. 14.

of Christ. The deacons have no authority at all. They are men and women chosen merely for doing the business of the church. Philippians 1:1, according to Nee, tells us exactly the organization of the church. It says, " . . . all the saints in Christ Jesus which are at Philippi, with the bishops and deacons."[6] Thus in the local church there are only two kinds of offices, that of the elders and that of the deacons.

Although Watchman Nee has professed to look down upon the ordering of God's truth into systems of theology as dead and non-lifegiving, almost every book he has written and every sermon he has preached is highly theological. In the same way, although he has spoken much against organization, yet his church is well organized. He has given very detailed instructions to his younger colleagues in matters of church organization, government, and administration.[7] He states in the introduction to *The Normal Christian Church Life* that missionary and organizational methods, although they should not be prized higher than the spiritual life of the individual believer and the life of the church, yet are as important as the wine-skin which holds the wine. It is essential to have good wine, yet it would be lost if there were no wine-skin to hold it.

With regard to membership Nee emphasizes the fact that any regenerated person who has accepted Jesus as Lord and Saviour is automatically a member of the local church. If there is any other requirement added for admission, immediately that church becomes a denomination. Who is within the circle and who is without the circle is determined by whether or not one has the indwelling of the Holy Spirit as taught in Romans 8:9.

On the practical side, problems arise because of the fact that Nee and his people do not recognize other sects

[6]Nee, *The Normal Christian Church Life.* p. 112.
[7]See both *Rethinking Our Missions* and *The Business of the Church.*

and denominations as the true local church. Lee tells us
that they are willing to consider those inside denominations as brothers and sisters in the Lord, who nevertheless
are wrong in having lost the ground of the local church.
They will have fellowship with these Christians but will
not trust them with responsibilities in service. This means
that such persons are not members of the true local church
of God. Their attitude towards those who do not recognize
the same basis for the local church is clearly seen in Lee's
nine-point manifesto.[8]

As we have pointed out before, Nee sees the nature
of the visible church as intensely local. There should be
one, and only one, church in any one locality. But one
runs into difficulties in management of large congregations in modern big cities. It is usually impossible and
inconvenient for all the Christians in such large localities
to assemble in one place for meetings. Nee suggests that
in a large city the church should be divided into districts,
with each one holding meetings in its separate place
(usually a house). The church in Jerusalem was probably
doing this even in its early days. We are told that they
held separate prayer meetings in different homes. Mark's
home was one example. Acts 2:46 also tells us that they
broke bread "from house to house." As to the size of
each district assembly, Nee suggests either fifty or one
hundred strong. He gets these numbers from Jesus' feeding of the five thousand. Jesus divided the multitude into
rows of fifty and a hundred. However, he does not regard
these numbers used by our Lord as mandatory. They
are merely a convenient guide.[9] At times for certain meetings and conventions all the district assemblies could
gather together for a joint meeting. Witness Lee seems
to suggest a larger district meeting. He further suggests
that the district, for the convenience of management,

[8]See pp. 90,91.
[9]Nee, *The Business of the Church*, p. 149.

should be divided into smaller groups of from twenty
to fifty people.[10] Each district has its own elders and
deacons, and the groups have group leaders called responsible brothers and sisters. This is how Nee and Lee have
their local churches structured and organized.

The main objective of the church is to lead brothers
and sisters into service. One doctrine Nee gives special
stress is the priesthood of all saints. Thus the church
must by all means make sure that every believer is
involved in service. For Nee, a church is no church until
all believers are involved in service. He points out five
kinds of service in which all believers in a church should
involve themselves. First is the work of evangelism. The
second is the work of follow-up of new converts prior
to baptism. The third is visitation of these new converts.
The fourth is what Nee calls "business visitation," the
giving of help to brothers and sisters when they have
difficulties like sickness and family problems, funerals
and weddings. The last is the care for brothers and sisters
who either have just arrived from a distant place or have
moved to another place.

For the building up of believers Nee suggests seven
types of meetings:

(1) Evangelistic meetings.
(2) Training courses for new converts.
(3) Fellowship meetings structured according to I Corinthians 14.
(4) Prayer meetings.
(5) The breaking of bread.
(6) Women's fellowship.
(7) Children's meetings.[11]

We notice in the above list that there is no Sunday morning

---

[10]Witness Lee, *An Outline of the Training Course for Service* (Taiwan:
Gospel Book Room), p. 87.

[11]Nee, *loc. cit.,* pp. 101–106.

worship service. Nee actually advocated the abolition of this type of service. We shall have more to say on this in our discussion on the worship of the church.[12]

Witness Lee, however, adds a few more items to this list of meetings. Besides the above seven, he lists:

(1) Regular Sunday service.

(2) A systematic series of message on one weekday evening every week.

(3) On another weekday evening every week, a series of messages for the deepening of the spiritual life.

(4) Bible studies (not weekly).

(5) Special meetings for the pursuit of growth of spiritual life.

(6) Summer and winter conferences.[13]

Most of the meetings mentioned above will be treated in detail in the section on church worship.[14] They are given here simply for the sake of giving the reader an over-all view of the organization of Nee's local church. In view of this, the repetition is deemed necessary.

Nee divides the work of the church into two types, that of the universal church and that of the local church. The work of the universal church is done by the "apostle" who goes out to found churches. These local churches are ruled by elders appointed by the "apostles." However the "apostle" has no authority over the elders and the local church. Nee advocates a clear-cut separation between the "apostolic" work and the work of the local church. But there is of course, a cyclical relationship between the local church and the work ("apostolic" work): the work produces local churches directly, while the local churches produce workers and work indirectly.

The "apostles," or what Nee calls "workers," have the responsibility of founding local churches, while the main

[12]See pp. 119–122.
[13]Lee, *loc. cit.*, pp. 83–86.
[14]See pp. 119–122.

task of the local church is the building up of believers. The local church is involved in conducting meetings, such as local gospel-preaching meetings, prayer meetings, bread-breaking meetings, Bible-study meetings, meetings for the exercise of spiritual gifts, and so on. Nee sees no Scriptural warrant for the local church to be involved in other types of work such as schools, hospitals, orphanages, or even foreign missionary work.[15] These Nee considers works of faith and feels they should be run by individual believers. These separate works, like that of the "apostles," should not be thought of as part of the work of the local church, even though they contribute to the strengthening of the local church.

We observe from the previous discussion that, in Nee's concept, the church in a particular locality is a spontaneous association of believers who work together under the headship of Christ and the presidency of the Holy Spirit to build up the Body of Christ with fellowship and service. But the organization of the church is not spontaneous. Rather, it is structured according to the will of Christ in the Scriptures as interpreted by the Holy Spirit. The priesthood of all saints means the total involvement by all believers in all kinds of church activities. This implies the denunciation of the Roman Catholic priestly mediatorial system and the Protestant ministerial system.

Church Offices

According to Watchman Nee and his associates there are two kinds of workers who are involved in the building of the universal church and the local church. On the universal church level God sends four kinds of men: the apostles, the prophets, the evangelists, and the pastors

[15]Nee, *Rethinking Our Missions.* p. 227.

and teachers. The apostles and prophets lay the foundation while the evangelists and the pastor-teachers do the work of building up after the foundation is laid. These four types of workers are God's gifts to the universal church. For the local church, God sets up two kinds of offices, that of the elders and that of the deacons.

We have already noted the differences among the four worker-gifts God sends to the universal church.[16] Since Nee, however, places great emphasis on the office and ministry of the apostles, we must devote more space to adequately treat Nee's concept of the apostles' work.

Apostles

Nee sees the office of the apostles as the highest among all church workers. This is indicated by the place it occupies at the head of the list of offices, both in I Corinthians 12:28 and in Ephesians 4:11. Apostles are specially sent by God to found churches in all places. Their sphere of work includes the preaching of the gospel, mediating revelation from God to His people, the decision on the form and doctrine of the church, the building up of saints, and the distribution of the gifts.[17] Thus it is obvious to see why Nee assigns to them the highest and most important positions in the church of God.

What constitutes a person an apostle is not his gifts but the simple fact that he is commissioned by God. An apostle might have the gift of prophecy or teaching, yet these do not make him an apostle. Apostleship is an office and not a personal gift. That the meaning of an apostle is simply "a sent one" is amply borne out not merely by its meaning in Greek, but also by what the Bible says in Luke 11:49, "Therefore also said the wisdom of God, I will send them prophets and apostles, and some of them they shall slay and persecute." The apostles here were

[16]See pp. 77–80.
[17]Nee, *The Normal Christian Church Life*, p. 19.

not the Twelve. The context indicates that it was after the rejection of these earlier apostles and prophets that God sent His Son. This indicates that all the prophets sent by God to His people were apostles, but in an Old Testament sense.

The first apostle in the New Testament was not one of the Twelve but our Lord Himself. He is the Great Apostle (Hebrews 3:1). Then Christ appointed His twelve apostles. These men do occupy a special position in the Kingdom of God as witnesses to the resurrection of our Lord. They were chosen from the many disciples of our Lord to do His work (Luke 6:13). They were to sit on thrones with Christ to judge the twelve tribes of Israel (Luke 22:30). Thus they occupy a special and distinctive position in the eternal plan of God which later apostles do not have.

The Holy Spirit also called men to be apostles after the ascension of Christ. These, though they could not be ranked among Christ's twelve, yet were apostles. The apostles mentioned in Ephesians 4 were appointed by the Holy Spirit after Christ's ascension and were commissioned to build up the Body of Christ. The first instance of the Holy Spirit's sending apostles is found in Acts 13, when Paul and Barnabas were sent out on their missionary journey. Besides Paul and Barnabas there are other Holy Spirit–commissioned apostles in the New Testament. As Nee understands the verse, Paul refers to Titus as an apostle in II Corinthians 8:23. Andronicus and Junia are spoken of as noted apostles (Romans 16:7), says Nee. In I Corinthians 15 both the Twelve and other apostles are mentioned together as having seen the resurrected Lord: In verse 5 Cephas and the Twelve are mentioned; then in verse 7 He is said to have been seen by James and all the apostles. And in II Corinthians 11:13 we learn that there were false apostles. Finally Nee points out that there were even women apostles in the Bible.

According to him, a certain Greek authority thinks that Junia is a woman's name (Romans 16:7). Thus for him there is overwhelming evidence for the existence of apostles after the Twelve.

Nee is very careful in defining the relationship between the "work" of the apostle and the local church.[18] According to him the "work"[19] and the local church are two distinct, separate organized entities. The "work" of the apostle is never part of the local church. The apostles have no authority over the local church at all. All the authority in the local church rests on the elders. When an apostle goes to a meeting of the local church he is just another brother. Like what Paul did to the Corinthian church, an apostle can advise the local church in doing certain things and make recommendations. Yet the apostle has only spiritual authority over the local church and not formal administrative authority. Even when the elders act contrary to the advice of the apostle, they are only wrong spiritually, not formally. What Paul did when he was in Rome provides a good example for all apostles. He rented his own house and preached the gospel there for two years although there was already in existence a strong local church.

With regard to the relationship between the local church and the apostle, there are three things that the workers should bear in mind:

(1) The "work" is the special concern of the workers, not of the churches, and the sphere of any work is not wide enough to justify its being regarded as a church.

(2) All workers must be humble enough to take the place of brothers in the local church. In the sphere of their work they hold the position of God's servants, but in the sphere of the church they are only brethren.

[18]Nee, *Rethinking Our Missions.* pp. 222–253.
[19]"Work" is the word used by Nee to mean the ministry of the apostle.

(3) The goal of all work is the establishment of local churches. If we make our work the basis of a separate unit of God's people, then we are building up a sect, not a church.[20]

The relationship between workers is also important to Nee.[21] The New Testament workers did not organize themselves into a mission. Yet this did not mean they had no connection with one another of any sort. We see Paul, Luke, Silas, Timothy, Titus, and Apollos always working together, whereas Peter, James, and John formed another group. We also see that when Christ sent out His apostles, they went out two by two. Thus this kind of free, informal association of workers is ordained by our Lord.

There was no deliberate organization among the workers. It was only a spontaneous fellowship and coordination created and begun by the Holy Spirit. The apostles did not choose their own company on a partisan or doctrinal basis. The Holy Spirit commanded the church in Antioch to separate for Him Barnabas and Saul. The apostles of Christ also did not choose their own company to go out. The Lord appointed them two by two.

Although there was no organization among workers, yet there was spiritual authority and leadership. The following Scripture references demonstrate this fact clearly: Acts 15:36–40; 16:10; 17:15; 20:3–5, 13,14; I Corinthians 16:10–12; II Corinthians 8:6, 16–18, 22,23; Ephesians 6:21–22; Philippians 2:19,25; Colossians 4:7, 14, 17; I Thessalonians 3:1,2; II Timothy 4:9–13, 20,21; Titus 1:5; 3:12,13.

These verses show that Paul was the leader among his group of workers. He had authority to send certain workers to a certain place or to leave some of his younger colleagues at a certain place. Seniority here is not based

[20]Nee, *The Normal Christian Church Life*. p. 84.
[21]*Ibid*.. pp. 85–96.

on an election by the church, but on spiritual growth. It is a spiritual authority and not an official one. This authority is spontaneous and readily recognized by others, as when Peter on the day of Pentecost stood up to speak for his fellow apostles, and on other occasions later. Yet again it should be recognized that there was no central control as such. This was only fellowship. Why is it so important that a group of workers should function spontaneously as a body and not as an organization? Nee offers some good reasons:

> The explanation is this: God does not wish the power of organization to take the place of the power of the Holy Spirit. A good organization often serves as a poor substitute for the power of the Holy Spirit, by holding a work together even after all its vitality is gone. When life has departed from the work and the scaffolding of organization still supports it, its collapse is prevented; but that is doubtful gain, for a splendid outward organization may be blinding God's servants to a deep inward need. God would rather His work be discontinued than that it go on with such a counterfeit for spiritual power. When the glory of God had departed from the temple He Himself left it to utter ruin.[22]

There might be different groups engaging in different ministries for the Lord. Among these various companies there should be fellowship and cooperation. They should all function as one body. The guiding principle, once again, is: one body, under the headship of Jesus Christ and the superintendency of the Holy Spirit.

The principle of "one church at one locality" is also important for the workers. This means that the supreme aim of all workers should be the founding and building of local churches. In other words, the worker must not start a church of his own at a locality where the church of God already exists.

[22]*Ibid.*, pp. 91–92.

With regard to financial matters, Nee believes in total dependence on God by faith for support of the workers and the work. They should go to God for their financial needs and not to the local church or any man.[23] To draw a salary from the local church or any other church organization involves the danger of being directed and manipulated by the organization. There are two proper ways for an apostle to support himself and his work. The one is to look to God by faith and the other is to take a part-time job.

It is our Lord's principle that "the labourer is worthy of his hire" (Luke 10:7). Following the same principle, Paul also reiterates that "even so hath the Lord ordained that they which preach the gospel should live of the gospel" (I Corinthians 9:14). To live of the gospel does not mean to receive a regular salary from the church. Nee states the principle this way:

> What it does mean is that the preachers of the Gospel may receive gifts from the brethren, but no stipulations are made in connection with such gifts. No definite period of time is named, no definite sum of money, no definite responsibility; all is a matter of free will.[24]

Yet Nee warns that not all gifts are to be received. The giver should consider it as giving to God; and the receiver should receive it as receiving it for the Lord. Thus any money given without the right spiritual motivation should not be received. That is why Paul received from the Philippians and not from the Corinthians. It is obvious from this that, as taught in III John 7, the worker should not receive any money from non-believers.

Nee is also careful in exhorting the local churches to support workers, although it is not their formal and official duty to send money on a regular and permanent basis.

[23]Nee, *Rethinking Our Missions,* p. 257 ff.
[24]Nee, *The Normal Christian Church Life,* p. 100.

Workers should also help each other financially. When the need arises the worker should always be ready to take a secular part-time job to support his own needs. Paul's tent-making is a good example. But it must always be remembered that all is done for the sake of the work.

Elders

As Nee sees it in the Bible, the authority in the local church is placed in the hands of the elders. They are in charge of governing, overseeing, teaching and pastoring. They are the ones who make the final decisions in all church matters for the deacons to carry out.

The word "elder" is taken from the Old Testament.[25] The Israelites had elders in their cities. The Gospels also mention these Israelite elders. Even in the first part of Acts the elders mentioned there are also Old Testament elders (Acts 4:5, 8, 23; 6:12). The elders of the New Testament church were first found in the Jerusalem church.

Elders are to be appointed by apostles on the basis of spiritual maturity and never of administrative ability. And of course, the original apostles did not choose on the basis of their own likes. They only ordained those whom God had already ordained (Acts 20:28). Also, these elders were not suddenly brought out of obscurity to a leading position. They were already prominent in the church as people filled with the Holy Spirit, gifted, and already displaying spiritual leadership. The qualifications for the eldership are those stated in both Titus 1:6–9 and I Timothy 3:2–7.

Nee believes in a plurality of elders. According to him every local church should have more than one elder.[26] The one-man-rule system is not found in the Bible. It easily leads to pride and dictatorial practices.

The elders are the ones who oversee the work and

---

[25]Nee, *Rethinking Our Missions*. p. 102.
[26]*Ibid.*. p. 114.

service of church members. Thus they do not do work for others. In Nee's words, elders are not "a group of men who contract to do the church work on behalf of its members." They only direct and supervise the church in her work.

As stated before, the elders concern themselves with both the administrative side and spiritual side of things. Yet the governing of the church is their primary duty. In ruling, the elder is not to display the attitude of a dictator. He is not to bind but to set an example (I Peter 5:3). He should work with the brothers and sisters.

According to Nee, the elders can also be apostles. There are examples in the Bible as we see in Peter and John. They went out as apostles; but when they returned they could no longer exercise the authority of apostles. They were elders with the status of a brother in the local church.

The Council of Jerusalem gives Nee the best model for business discussion and decision making in the church. First of all, the person directly involved in a controversial matter can give his report and express his feelings. Then let those who are qualified testify to the facts. After that all church members present can voice all their opinions. All members who desire to speak should be heard and all opinions should be taken into consideration, because the Holy Spirit may speak through any member. Finally, after they have expressed all their opinions, let the most advanced spiritual leader make the decision. The decision made must be one that seems "good to the Holy Spirit and to us." Witness Lee discerns four basic points in decision making:

(1) The feeling of the church.
(2) God's activity.
(3) God's Word.
(4) Spiritual authority.[27]

[27]Lee, *An Outline of the Training Course for Service.* p. 82.

Nee concludes his discussion on the church's business meeting by saying:

> Therefore I wish that brothers could see that the way the church goes about doing her business is neither dictatorial nor democratic. There is no room for despotism, neither is there room for democracy. Nothing should be settled by the opinion of one man, or by voting. The final decision making in the church is always in the hands of those who possess spiritual authority. But everybody should be given an opportunity to speak. Let them speak and you listen, trying to feel the movement of the Spirit, until you can finally stand up and say, "Brothers, the few of us have decided on this matter." In the church there is no such a thing as the minority obeying the majority or vice versa. In the church we have only brothers and sisters expressing their opinion, leaving the authority to decide to those who have attained spiritual maturity. After the decision is made, the whole church should dedicate themselves with one accord to carry it out. This is different from all methods of worldly organizations. I hope brothers and sisters can see this.[28]

Deacons

Nee compares the work of the deacons to that of the Levites in the Old Testament.[29] While the priests took charge of the spiritual matters, the Levites were responsible for the business matters. Thus the deacons of the New Testament church are those who take care of the business of the church. They are administrators who carry out what the elders have decided.

Whereas there is a plurality of elders in the local church, there should also be a plurality of deacons, as the Bible indicates (Philippians 1:1, I Timothy 3:8,12).[30] Not only should there be more than one deacon, the number should also always exceed that of the elders. The number of deacons is also determined by needs. A larger church

[28]Nee, *The Business of the Church,* pp. 179, 180.
[29]*Ibid.,* p. 61.
[30]Lee, *The Ministry of the Word,* LVII–LXI, p. 1080.

needs more deacons and a smaller one needs less.

While there should be only male elders in the local church because they are, on the human level, the head of the church, there can be both male and female deacons. In the New Testament we have both men (I Timothy 3:12) and women (I Timothy 3:11-margin; Romans 16:1) chosen to be deacons.

The appointment of deacons is done the same way as the appointment of elders. The apostles are supposed to appoint only those the Holy Spirit has already appointed. The qualifications of deacons are as recorded in I Timothy 3:8–13.

Church Ordinances

Most Protestant churches recognize only two ordinances that Christians should observe: baptism and the Lord's Supper. Witness Lee and his group add two more of these outward rites to be administered in the church, the laying on of hands and the veiling of women.[31] As to the meaning of these signs of reverence, Lee has these important words to say:

> As a matter of fact these are not mere ceremonies and regulations. They are practical steps and actual procedures through which we accept, receive, and enjoy the salvation of God and accompanying blessings.[32]

Thus for Lee these are not just signs which express and demonstrate certain invisible truths. He comes very close to the Romanist view of sacraments which actually confer grace and produce holiness. We shall see more

---

[31]While the "Little Flock" undoubtedly practiced these rites from the beginning, they are not discussed in Nee's writings.

[32]Witness Lee, "Baptism," *The Ministry of the Word.* XI (July, 1952), p. 178.

of this emphasis as we discuss one by one these four ordinances as practiced by Lee.

Nee, on the other hand, has had little to say about church ordinances (see pages 44 and 54). But to my knowledge, no one who knows Nee has ever accused him of heresy in these matters.

Baptism

As is usual in Witness Lee's Biblical and systematic treatment of doctrines, he begins his discussion of this doctrine by pointing out its importance. His first point is that if even Jesus was careful in fulfilling this requirement, how much more should we do the same. "It becometh us to fulfill all righteousness," says Jesus (Matthew 3:15). Jesus also indicates that the non-observance of this rite is the abolition of God's will and His plan (Luke 7:30). In His famous discourse with Nicodemus, Jesus declares that one must be born of both water and spirit. Water here for Lee means baptism. It is thus an important procedure for regeneration. Jesus always connects faith with baptism (Mark 16:16). Peter also thinks of it as of equal importance with belief and repentance for the remission of sins (Acts 2:37, 38, 41). In the case of the Ethiopian eunuch we see that the first thing he did immediately after his conversion was to get out of his carriage and get baptized. The Holy Spirit did not take Philip away until the rite was completed. Lee also cites the cases of Paul, the Philippian jailer, Cornelius and others to show that the first and immediate thing to be done to a new convert is to baptize him. Lastly, in the great commission Jesus also tells us that it is an important thing to be done in our missionary work.

Lee next treats the relationship between baptism and salvation. It is unbiblical, he says, to hold that baptism has nothing to do with our salvation. Quoting and explaining John 3:5, which says ". . . except a man be born of water and of the spirit, he cannot enter the kingdom of God," Lee says:

> Our Lord tells us here, in order to gain an entrance into the Kingdom of God not only do we need to be born of the Spirit, we also have to be born of water. We have already seen that what our Lord refers to as "born of water" is water baptism. Therefore water baptism results in a man's being born again into the Kingdom of God. It is a requirement for one's gaining regeneration. Of course this does not mean only the outward symbol. It has more to do with the inner reality of water baptism. Yet we cannot consider all reality as spiritual, and so say it does not need to be practiced. In the same manner that we ought to repent and believe in order to gain life from our Lord through the Holy Spirit, we ought to go through the rite of baptism by which we bring everything that belongs to ourselves to an end.[33]

Thus we see that according to Lee we must go through the rite of water baptism in order to gain salvation, just as much as we have to repent and believe. He also makes a woodenly literal interpretation of baptism in all instances when it is connected with salvation. Thus when Ananias told Paul to "arise, and be baptized, and wash away thy sins" (Acts 22:16), he means that baptism can actually wash away our sins. When Peter asked the converts to be baptized in the name of Jesus Christ for the remission of sins at Pentecost, he means the same thing. He laid out three conditions for the remission of sins as (1) repentance, (2) belief in the name of the Lord, and (3) water baptism. Peter also tells us that water baptism does save us (I Peter 3:21). Lee also points out that in Mark 16:16 our Lord's command is: "He that believeth and is baptized shall be saved" and not "He that believes and is saved shall be baptized," as many have so "twisted and inter-

---

[33]*Ibid.*, p. 182.

preted" the saying. Also, when Paul says in Romans 6 that we were baptized into His death, he means that water baptism is the procedure by which we actually enter into this death and resurrection experience of Christ.

This leads Lee to the discussion of the meaning of water baptism. It is first of all a procedure for gaining union with Christ, as Romans 6:3 indicates. More specifically, we are united with Him in His death, burial, and resurrection. This death separates us from our old selves and the world. The resurrection makes us new creatures, able to partake of all the blessings of Christ. I Peter 3:21, according to Darby's translation, means that baptism creates in us the witness of a blameless conscience. This is a witness to the angels, good and fallen, and all creatures.

As to the meaning of the Greek word *baptisma,* Lee quotes Luther, Calvin, and Stanley to argue that it is immersion. The examples of Jesus' "coming out of the water" and that of the eunuch's "going into the water" also prove that immersion is the Biblical teaching.

New Testament baptism is prefigured in the Old Testament by Noah's ark in the flood and the Israelites' passage through the Red Sea (I Peter 3:20,21; I Corinthians 10:1,2). As Noah's being saved through the ark meant his separation from the world, so water baptism also takes us out of this world to belong to a new Kingdom. The passing through the Red Sea was also the necessary step in the leaving behind of the old world and all that was in it to enter the place of rest and blessedness. The Israelites had already expressed their faith with the passover lamb. Yet this faith was not enough; they must pass through the Red Sea. In like manner, it is not enough that we have faith to give us salvation; we must also pass through the Red Sea, so that we can break loose from the clutch of the enemy.

Those baptized are those who believe, as indicated in the Scripture (Mark 16:16; Acts 8:12, 37–39; 18:8); so infant baptism is unscriptural, because infants cannot believe.

It is also wrong to think that the performance of the rite is exclusively a privilege of the clergy. John 4:2 tells us that Jesus did not baptize; He asked His disciples to do it. Note here that Jesus did not ask only the apostles, who were to be officers of the church, to baptize. Paul also did not personally baptize the majority of his converts (I Corinthians 1:14–17). The following passages also show that it was the disciples, not just apostles, who did the baptizing: Matthew 28:19, Acts 9:10, 17,18. So the performance of baptism should not be made the exclusive right of the minister.

The Bible also shows clearly that all believers as soon as they believed were baptized, such as the believers at Pentecost, the eunuch, the Philippian jailer, and Cornelius. With regard to the place of baptism, Lee points out that it is any convenient place with enough water for immersion, as shown by the examples of John the Baptist (John 3:23) and Philip the Evangelist (Acts 8:36). Lee also suggests that those who have been baptized without understanding its true significance and those who were baptized as infants should be rebaptized. An example of rebaptism is furnished in Acts 19:3–5, when Paul rebaptized the Ephesian disciples.

In conclusion, I would like to quote Lee's definition of baptism:

> Therefore baptism is not a religious initiation rite or a ceremony. It is a practical procedure and an actual step taken out of faith, through which we enter into Christ, become united with Him, and receive in Him the complete salvation and a blameless conscience, a silent testimony of real action.[34],[35]

[34]*Ibid.*, p. 186.
[35]Lee's teaching on this subject will be analyzed in Chapter 5.

The Laying on of Hands

Another ordinance prescribed by the New Testament, according to Lee, is the laying on of hands. There are six fundamental doctrines as recorded in Hebrews 6:1,2 and the laying on of hands is one of them. But unlike the other five, this particular one is often ignored.

Lee goes back to the Old Testament to find the meaning of the laying on of hands. He sees that when Old Testament people performed sin offerings and burnt offerings they had to lay their hands on the animals. This means their identification and union with the animal, because atonement depends on the union of the sinner and the one that substitutes for him. Thus he concludes that the first meaning of this rite is identification and union.

In the twenty-seventh chapter of Numbers, we see God asked Moses to lay hands on Joshua in order to pass some of his honor on to the latter. This means communication and fellowship. Paul also laid hands upon Timothy to convey to him some gifts.

Thus the laying on of hands means both identification and communication. In II Kings 13:14–17, in the story of Elisha and the king, we see both meanings in Elisha's act.

Lee finds seven occasions for the laying on of hands. The first is for reception. This is done either after baptism or when publicly receiving somebody into the Body of Christ. The former is indicated by both Hebrews 6 and Acts 19:5,6. The latter is spoken of in Acts 8:16,17. Baptism is a personal rite and for a person's union with Christ; but the laying on of hands is for accepting a person into the Body of Christ.

The second occasion is the receiving of the Holy Spirit. The Apostles in Acts did this many times (Acts 8:16,17; 19:1–6; 9:17). In such acts those who represented the Body were able to communicate to the new believers the Holy Spirit that they already possessed.

Then there was the bestowing of gifts. This we have already seen in the case of Paul with Timothy.

The laying on of hands is also practiced when commissioning certain persons for doing certain things, as when the apostles laid hands on the seven deacons of the Jerusalem church. Yet Lee points out that this is not ordination but that it means only identification and communication.

The laying on of hands is also for the sending out of workers. The occasion mentioned immediately before pertained to a ministry in the church, while this one is for sending workers out to perform a certain job.

The bestowal of blessings is another occasion for the laying on of hands, as when our Lord blessed the little children that came to Him (Mark 10:13–16).

Finally there is the laying on of hands for healing the sick. Jesus did this, and also in His great commission told His disciples to do the same (Luke 4:40; Mark 16:18). When Paul did it in Acts 28:8 he was following Christ's example.

Lee concludes by pointing out that one should not lay on hands carelessly. It is a most serious and solemn matter, as taught in I Timothy 5:22 which says, "Lay hands suddenly on no man, neither be partaker of other men's sins; keep thyself pure." This is obvious when we realize that the laying on of hands means identification and communication. When we lay hands on a sinful, unworthy person we share with him his iniquities.

The Veiling of Women

Witness Lee holds that the use of a head covering by women in the church is another important rite for the New Testament church. Some think that since it is taught only by Paul (I Corinthians 11:2–16) it is only man's teaching, and not God's. Lee argues that this is not so, because Paul says in the Epistle to the Galatians that what he preaches is all revealed to him by the Lord (Galatians 1:11–12).

Some also argue that it is a Jewish custom. Yet Paul speaks very often of breaking with Jewish custom and practices. It would not be in keeping with his practice to advocate the keeping of a Jewish rite. Moreover, the Jewish practice is just the opposite of Paul's teaching of the veiling of women. It was not the women but the priests who, when they went before God, had to cover their heads.

Neither was it merely the culturally conditioned practice of the Corinthians, says Lee. Paul said he was writing to all the saints (I Corinthians 1:2). It was also a practice for all the churches, says Lee, as I Corinthians 11:16 indicates.

The meaning of veiling is stated by Paul in verse 10. It is a sign of authority over them. This means they are willing to submit to authority over them.

This rite is to express the sovereignty of God and the hierarchy of authority prescribed by Him. As stated in verses 3 and 4, the order is as follows: God is the head of Christ, Christ the head of the church, and men the head of women. This is an order ordained by God for the universe. The veiling of women is thus an acknowledgement and demonstration of this divine order. Yet this order is not concerned with the equality of the sexes any more than it has to do with the equality of God the Father and God the Son. It is a matter of different functions of men and women in God's predestined economy and involves subordination, not inferiority.

Paul tells us in verse 7 that it is also according to the different roles God has appointed men and women to play. Man is the image and glory of God and so represents God. For this reason man should not cover his head. Woman, on the other hand, is the glory of man and so represents him. This divine arrangement furnishes Paul with another basis for the doctrine.

This rite is also based on God's order of creation, as Paul points out in verses 8–12. God not only created man and woman with different roles to play, they were also created in a particular order, man first and woman last. Woman is also made for man and not man for woman. It is because of this that a woman should express submission with the covering on her head.

The fourth basis for this doctrine is stated in verse 10. It is done for the sake of the angels. This goes back to the fall of Satan and his followers. They defied the sovereignty of God. Not only that, they also corrupted mankind. Yet God recovered His Kingdom with the redemptive work of Christ and obtained His sovereign rule in the church. The veiling of women in the church is simply to demonstrate this fact: that what God did not get from some of the angels, He gets from the church.

The fifth basis is found in man's nature, as pointed out by Paul in verses 13–15. Our nature tells us that man should be in a leading position while woman should be submissive.

Who then should have their heads covered? Paul in verse 5 refers only to women who are praying or preaching. In other words, when they are dealing with spiritual matters. From this Lee infers that woman should also cover their heads when they fellowship with one another and when they speak to others about the gospel.

Lee also points out that the wearing of long hair could not be regarded as meeting the requirement of veiling, as verses 5 and 6 indicate. Since the head covering is to be put over the hair, Lee advocates that it must be big enough to cover all the hair.

The rite of veiling is prefigured in the Old Testament by the example of Rebekah. When she saw Isaac she covered herself with a veil. It is also a common custom from the most savage society to the most civilized society

that the bride during the wedding is supposed to cover
her head. This is a sign of submissiveness. When the
priests in the Old Testament went before God they also
covered their heads. This also prefigured the fact that
when touching matters of the spiritual realm the women
have to show the sign of submission.

The importance of this sign of reverence is clear when
we realize that the first half of I Corinthians 11 is devoted
to the discussion of this doctrine while the last half of
the chapter is used to treat the Lord's Supper. For Paul
the two rites are of equal importance. The first part of
the chapter deals with the head while the second part
deals with the body.

The Lord's Supper

Witness Lee goes into great detail in discussing the
Lord's Supper in I Corinthians. It was established by our
Lord Himself on the night when He was betrayed (I
Corinthians 11:23–25). It was also the night when they
ate the Passover meal. The Passover of the Old Testament,
a remembrance of God's salvation, symbolized the coming
Messiah. Now Christ was going to the cross to accomplish
the great redemptive work. Before the real thing that
the Passover signified came to pass, Jesus set up the
memorial supper to replace the Passover feast. As His
death fulfilled what the Passover prefigured, the breaking
of bread in the same manner replaced the Passover
remembrance.

The bread signifies, as Paul tells us, the body of Christ,
which was broken for us. In the Bible bread always represents life. Our Lord speaks of Himself as the "bread of
life" (John 6:35). Thus Christ died on the cross so that
we can receive life from God.

The cup in the Bible symbolizes a portion or a share
of something. Thus David in Psalm 16:5 says that the
Lord is the portion of his cup. As sinners our portion

before God should actually be the cup of His wrath (Revelation 14:10; 21:8). But God sent Christ to drink on the cross this cup of wrath for us (John 18:11). As a result of this He was able to give to us the cup of salvation as our cup of blessings (Psalm 116:13; 23:5). The blood is also the foundation for the establishment of the new covenant. Christ's blood, therefore, not only gives us a share in all the blessings of God, it also established a new covenant. It takes away our sins and at the same time brings us all the blessings of God.

The Supper is exclusively for the remembrance of our Lord as He commanded us to do (I Corinthians 11:23). The whole attention should be given to the meaning of His death as signified by the bread and the cup. Paul also tells us that the Supper is also for the enjoying of our Lord. He tells us that when we eat the bread and drink the cup we eat His body and His blood—we are enjoying Him who is in us spiritually.

The breaking of the bread is also an open demonstration and exhibition of the death of Christ in order that all creatures in heaven and on earth may see it.

The breaking of the bread is not only a memorial and a display; in its observance we also await the coming of the Lord. So in His invisible presence we wait for His visible presence.

On the one hand, the Supper is exclusively for the remembrance of the Lord; on the other hand it is also for fellowship. It is a participation in both the blood and body of Christ, as Paul tells us in I Corinthians 10:16, 21. It is first of all a fellowship between the Lord and the Christian. It is also a fellowship among Christians.

The Lord's Supper is also a testimony. It is a testimony of our union with Christ. When we eat the bread and drink the cup, it is a symbol of our dying and rising with our Lord. Then it is also a testimony of the unity of the church. Paul says, "For we being many are one

bread, and one body: for we are all partakers of that
one bread" (I Corinthians 10:17). Jesus was that one seed
which by dying produced many seeds. The Holy Spirit
was then able to make that one bread out of these many
seeds, which are the believers. Yet this unity signified
by the bread can be broken up by dissension and factions
in the church. This happened in the Corinthian church,
and it caused some of them to be sick and some even
to die.

What is the qualification for participation at the Lord's
Supper? Lee argues from the fact that Christ gave the
bread and the cup to the disciples that one must be a
believer in order to be qualified to participate (Matthew
26:26). Acts 2:44–46 also says that those who believed
broke bread together. It is also natural that only those
who have already received God's salvation can remember
the Lord at the Supper.

As for the time of the breaking of the bread, Lee points
out that in the beginning the disciples broke bread daily
(Acts 2:46). This implies that the more frequently it is
observed, the better. Later the early believers developed
a custom of observing it on the first day of the week
(Acts 20:7). It is only appropriate that we remember His
death on the day of His resurrection. Lee suggests that
it is best made an evening observance, because it is supposed to be a supper. Moreover, after a day of hard work
we feel relieved and relaxed in the evening. What time
is better for this kind of meeting than the evening?

Lee also notices that the early Christians broke bread
from house to house (Acts 2:46). Thus if it is not possible
to gather the whole local church for the Supper, it is
just as good to hold such meetings at different homes.

Lee concludes by pointing out three things for the
believer to do after observing the Lord's Supper. First,
he should long for the coming of the Lord (I Corinthians
11:26). Secondly, Paul says he cannot drink both the

cup of the Lord and the cup of demons, or partake of
the Lord's table as well as the table of demons (I
Corinthians 10:21). This means that after eating the Lord's
Supper we should not seek after the things of this world.
Lastly, Paul also exhorts us not to use the old leaven,
the leaven of malice and wickedness (I Corinthians 5:7–8).
This means that after the breaking of bread with other
believers one should rid himself of all corruption and
evils in his life in order to live a sanctified life.

The Meetings of the Church

As pointed out before, Watchman Nee denounces very
violently the Sunday morning worship service of the
Protestant church. This "pulpit-and-pew" type of meeting
causes the church to be stagnant for the believers become
mere passive receivers. The root of the whole problem
he believes, is the confusing of the apostolic meeting
with the church meeting. The kind of service we have
in the Protestant church, at which one man speaks and
all others listen, is not truly a church meeting at all; it
is, rather, an apostolic meeting. Mutuality is the nature
of the church, and so all the church meetings should
be based on the principle of mutual help and mutual
edification. This calls for a round-table type of meeting
at which each member seeks to contribute to the building
up of the whole Body.

Thus Nee divides meetings into two types, apostolic
and church.[36] Examples of the former are the meeting which
was held at Pentecost (Acts 2:14), the gathering in
Solomon's Porch (Acts 3:11), and that in Cornelius' house
(Acts 10:34).

With regard to church meetings, Nee finds four types

[36]Nee, *Normal Christian Church Life*, pp. 118, 119.

recorded in the Bible:

(1) Prayer meetings (Acts 2:42; 4:24,31; 12:5).

(2) Scripture reading meetings (Colossians 4:16; I Thessalonians 5:27; Acts 2:42; 15:21,30,31).

(3) Meetings for the breaking of bread (I Corinthians 10:16,17; Acts 2:42; 20:7).

(4) Meetings for the exercise of spiritual gifts (I Corinthians 14).

To the above list he adds the following:[37]

(5) Gospel-preaching meetings.

(6) Training courses for new converts.

(7) Women's fellowship meetings.

(8) Children's meetings.

The meeting that Nee puts most emphasis on is the gospel-preaching meeting of the local church. He gives careful instruction as to how this kind of meeting should be conducted. The guiding principle for this work of the local church is the mobilization of all believers. The objective is to work on the unbeliever until he becomes baptized. This he calls "gospel care."

He suggests that each Christian, when he comes to a gospel meeting, should bring no more than three or four friends, so that he can give them maximum care during and after the meeting. If one has more than four friends coming with him, then he should make arrangements with the brother in charge of the meeting to find others to take care of the extras.

During the meeting the believer should seat two non-believers on each side, so that he can help them to find the Scripture passages and hymns. He should also be very much in prayer during the whole session, both for his friends and the speaker.

The whole meeting should take one or two hours. Two-thirds of the time should be given to the "casting out

---

[37]Nee, *The Business of the Church*. pp. 101–116.

of the net," and one-third of the time to "drawing the net." At the time of net-drawing, the believer should attempt to persuade and urge his friends until they fall right into the net. After the meeting he should pray with them and get them registered for further follow-up work.

This is the kind of meeting that Nee used to replace the Sunday morning worship service—which, he says, is a traditional Romanist and Protestant custom which should be done away with because it is not a church meeting. He notes that as long as the Sunday pulpit is maintained the ministerial system has to be kept up too.

Chronologically, the training sessions for new converts come after the gospel meeting. The course is composed of fifty-two lessons for the fifty-two weeks of the year. Each believer should encourage and make sure that the new convert he is in charge of practices what is taught in the lessons. When the new convert misses a lesson, the believer should go to his home to give the "make-up" lesson. Nee states the importance of the training meeting as follows:

> The strength of the training session determines the strength of the next generation. When it is weak the next generation will also be weak. No doubt they have all believed in the gospel and have all been saved, but there is no church. It is just like an evangelistic meeting. There is evangelism and results, but there is no church.[38]

For believers the most important meeting is the fellowship meeting, fashioned after I Corinthians 14. As pointed out before, the basic principle at such meetings is mutual help and edification. Dangers at such meetings include confusion, disorganization, and lengthiness. Thus it is important that the brother in charge should take full control of the meeting, encouraging one to speak more and persuading another tactfully to be brief. He should be

[38]*Ibid.,* p. 104.

able to discern the working of the Spirit at the meeting and be able to manage the proceedings accordingly.

In passing, it should be pointed out that Nee allows women to give testimonies at such meetings if the brother in charge invites them to do so.

As to prayer meetings, Nee gives three suggestions. First, the prayers must be brief. Second, they must be sincere. We must pray so that God can hear and not, primarily, so that others might hear. Prayer is not for teaching brothers and sisters the truth, as some are fond of doing in their public prayers. Lastly, the meeting should concentrate on praying for one item. It is good sometimes to spend a whole session praying for just one sick brother. Or, it could be devoted to praying for all the sick in the church. Even when there are many prayer requests, they should not be announced beforehand. Believers ought to pray for one item thoroughly and then the responsible brother should announce the next item.

Nee divides the Lord's Supper into two parts. The first part is for the worship and praise of the Son, and the second is for the worship of the Father. The first part constitutes the Supper proper. Then in the second part the believers should worship and praise the Father for the manifold blessings He has brought to us through His Son.

As to the time for the different types of meetings, Nee suggests that the gospel meeting be held on Sunday morning and the training sessions and meetings geared to the building up of believers be held on Thursday or Friday. Saturday is reserved for fellowship meetings of the I Corinthians 14 type.

In conclusion, it must be observed that Nee and his followers take great pains in attempting to structure their local churches exactly as the New Testament teaches. Whether or not such an approach is called for by Scripture we shall discuss in the next chapter.

Chapter 5

EVALUATION AND CONCLUSION

A Critique of Nee's Ecclesiology

Watchman Nee's ecclesiology, as we have seen, is derived from the teaching of the Brethren Movement and his own insight into Biblical teaching. The Brethren Movement triggered in him a new interest in a fresh understanding and approach to the doctrine of the church, and led him to search more deeply into the Bible for guidance in church life and practice. He earnestly believes that a careful investigation of the New Testament will yield a complete and definite system of church government and practice. Regarding the New Testament as a normative basis of church polity, Nee rejects the Roman Catholic system, the Protestant practice, and even the Brethren formulation. In his thinking, tradition and expediency have no place in determining church polity, and thus must be rejected.

The Reformation principle of *Sola Scriptura* does definitely require us to regard the Bible as the normative guide for faith and practice. The Roman Church is thus wrong in putting tradition and the authority of the Church on a par with or above the teaching of the Bible. It is equally wrong for some Protestant groups to put aside Scriptural principles and, working on the expediency premise, rely on divine providence to guide in the development of church polity. We must accept the New Testament as the authoritative source of church polity. Yet the adoption of a Scriptural basis for church practice does not of itself necessarily exclude use of either tradition or expediency in the formulation of policies for church life.

Nee sees the Protestant ministerial system and the Sunday morning service as more of a Protestant traditional heritage than a Biblical practice. He thus has advocated their abolition. Denominationalism, too, is a tradition and a vice. It also, therefore, must go. Working on this principle, Nee has eliminated many otherwise advantageous practices. We should realize, however, that tradition *does* have a proper place in the formulation of church life, although it must always be subordinate to Scriptural principles, which it must never violate. When it is rightly related to the fundamental basis of Scripture, it can be very helpful. The light of church history is of immense value in providing a better church program. The Sunday worship service was established because of the Christians' felt need to worship God and is, of course, a valuable traditional practice. In fact, Nee has not been able to do away with the Sunday worship service; the "Little Flock" still retains it. Likewise, the ministerial system *per se* is not against Scriptural principle. The Bible does have teaching elders called pastors. Other current practices like the choir, congregational hymn-singing, the Sunday School, and many other church activities are not found in the Bible—and yet they are useful and not against Scriptural principles. Such elements of our traditional heritage ought certainly to be utilized in serving the purposes of the church.

Like tradition, expediency too has its place in determining the style of church life. If we wish to make our religion relevant to a particular culture, in a particular age, we must make innovations and adopt new methods in church organization so as to make its ministry in the particular situation effective. Again, of course, we must not allow the principle of expediency to become an overriding or determinative criterion in our ecclesiology. Its operation must not be in opposition to explicit Biblical principles. But certain church offices—such as the assistant pastor, the Christian education director, and the treasurer—are not found in the Bible; yet these are necessary for the effective ministry of the church. Any attempt (such as Nee's and Lee's) to go back to the New Testament and rebuild the church exactly like the New Testament church in every detail will result in many problems and inconveniences—because a new situation in a new age demands a different type of approach.

Dargan, one of the greatest authorities in ecclesiology among Baptists, is right when he says: "The proper method of a study of ecclesiology is a combination of the Scriptural, historical and practical."[1]

The above discussion leads us to another important question: Does the New Testament contain a single consistent plan of church activity that we must follow slavishly? It is Nee's conviction that as in the Old Testament God granted an exact blueprint to His people for the construction of the tabernacle and the temple, so likewise in the New Testament God has also prescribed a definite pattern for the establishment and organization of the church. Any departure from this apostolic pattern is a perversion of His divine plan. This leads him to conclude that we must follow the principle of "one church at one locality," that denominationalism is completely wrong, and that every recorded practice of the apostolic church must be emphasized; in short, that a church is not a church unless it is established on the proper principle of "one locality, one church."

It is true, as we have already seen, that the Bible is the highest authoritative source of our church polity. Yet

---

[1]H. E. Dana, *A Manual of Ecclesiology* (Kansas City: Central Seminary Press, 1944), p. 211.

one must also realize that while there is a general pattern for the church in the New Testament, this Scriptural norm does not impose detailed and mechanical rules. There are only broad and essential principles given. In the Old Testament we find specific and detailed civil, ceremonial, and moral laws prescribed by God for His people to follow. In the New Testament the main emphasis is on basic vital principles, the specific guidance of the Holy Spirit within these principles, and Christian liberty controlled by love. This new spirit pervades all of Paul's writings. Thus to the Christians in Rome he said:

> One man regards one day above another, another regards every day alike. Let each man be fully convinced in his own mind. He who observes the day, observes it for the Lord, and he who eats, does so for the Lord, for he gives thanks to God; and he who eats not, for the Lord he does not eat, and gives thanks to God.[2]

Again to the Christians in Colosse he said:

> If you have died with Christ to the elementary principles of the world, why, as if you were living in the world, do you submit yourself to decrees, such as "Do not handle, do not taste, do not touch!" (which all refer to things destined to perish with the using)—in accordance with the commandments and teachings of men? These are matters which have, to be sure, the appearance of wisdom in self-made religion and self-abasement and severe treatment of the body, but are of no value against fleshly indulgence.[3]

Nee's attempt to reconstruct what the Bible reports often leads him to misuse scriptures. Thus the remark that Jesus went to all the "cities and villages" to preach the gospel is used by him as a guideline for definition of a locality. The fact that Jesus divided the five thousand into rows of fifty and one hundred is used as a guideline

[2]Romans 14:5,6 NASV
[3]Colossians 2:20–23 NASV

for determining the size of a district assembly. And the passage which states that Paul, while in Rome under house arrest, rented a dwelling from which he preached the gospel, is used by Nee to establish the two important principles that the work of the apostle has absolutely nothing to do formally with the work of the local church and that the apostle cannot officially demand support from the local church. Again, the incident of the dispersion of Christians from Jerusalem is used by him as the basis for evangelism by emigration.

It is true that the Bible is full of examples and experiences for us to follow. Yet we must not follow every recorded practice, but use careful discrimination. Some of the disciples in the early days practiced communal living. This example, obviously, is not meant to be followed generally. It should be noted in this regard that believers of the next generation did not follow their example, probably recognizing that what had been done was done simply out of expediency. But the "Little Flock" was following this example when they gave their businesses to the church in 1948. So it is important to realize that what is descriptive in the Bible is not necessarily normative.

During the apostolic age the church was experiencing changes and development, and therefore we cannot find a consistent, single plan of church activity in the book of Acts. The disciples still worshiped in the temple while they prayed and broke bread in the houses. Deacons were later elected when the need for some brethren to minister to the widows arose. Throughout the New Testament we find a wide variety in the practices of church life in different localities. Yet this does not mean that the New Testament is not normative in forming our church polity. How then can we formulate our ecclesiology according to the New Testament? H. E. Dana provides us with a useful guideline:

> Church life in Corinth was not precisely what it was in

Philippi, nor was church polity in Asia in exact harmony
with that reflected in the history of primitive Christianity
in Galatia. Nevertheless, the underlying principles of church
life and activity which we have observed as essential to the
conservation and promotion of redemptive experience operated throughout all the varieties of apostolic church polity.
Everywhere in apostolic life church government was democratic and autonomous. Nowhere does sacerdotalism or extreme
ritualism appear. An unbiased consideration of the New Testament leads to the conclusion that sacramentarianism had
not appeared when Christianity emerged into the second century. New Testament church polity was simple, spontaneous,
democratic. These vital principles are characteristic throughout the variations that may be observed.[4]

It took the church over a thousand years to recognize
and correct the wrong ecclesiastical practices of the
Roman Catholic Church. Under the principle of *Sola
Scriptura* the Protestant segment of Christendom has been
searching for a Biblical church polity. Different groups
have come to radically different conclusions from the
Bible. This has led to divisions and sometimes confusion.
Even among the Brethren group, whom Nee considers to
have arrived at a truly genuine Biblical pattern of church
government and practice, men were soon divided because
of the different aspects of truth they saw. Doesn't this
fact of church history tell us that it is harmful and futile
to construct a certain pattern of church activity and then
claim it to be the only Biblical pattern? Shouldn't Nee
and Lee and the "Little Flock" consider their pattern as
only one of the Biblical patterns which has found favor
with God and has been used by Him? A failure to see
this has led the "Little Flock" to be more and more exclusive and more and more hostile to other church groups.
Yet both those who "esteem one day as better than
another" and those who "esteem all days alike" are equally

[4]Dana, *op. cit.*, pp. 206,207.

accepted by God, provided they both aim at doing it for the glory of God.

The starting point of Nee's doctrine of the local church is the assumption that denominationalism is sin. It is said to be the cause of the stagnation, confusion, and backwardness that have plagued the Protestant church for the past few centuries, and must be done away with. The only solution, Nee supposes, is to return to the Biblical ground of "one church at one locality." Since it is impossible for the denominational churches as a whole to dissolve their organizations and return to this Biblical principle, Nee urges individual Christians to leave such evil establishments to join the local church which *is* operated under the Biblical principle of "one church at one locality."

Nee cites Galatians 5, I Corinthians 1 and 11 to show that denominationalism is a sin condemned by the Bible. That dissension which leads to parties is a sin of the flesh no one can deny (Galatians 5:20). But had this quarreling produced actual sects or denominations within the churches? No. According to the great New Testament commentator Henry Alford—with whose commentary Nee is familiar and whose opinion Nee respects—the word *haireseis* (heresies, factions, cliques), the word under discussion in I Corinthians 11:19 and Galatians 5:20, refers to those who choose "their self-willed line and adhere to it."[5] He further states that the primary meaning is not an ecclesiastical one. As to the passage in the first chapter of I Corinthians, Alford again warns us that we must not infer that there were four different quarrelsome parties or denominations existing in the church of Corinth. Commenting on I Corinthians 1:12 he says:

> Respecting the matter of fact to which the verse alludes, I have given reference in the Prology. 11.10, to the principal

---

[5]Henry Alford, *The Greek Testament* (Chicago: Moody Press, 1968), III, p. 59.

theories of the German critics, and will only here restate the conclusions which I have there endeavoured to substantiate: (1) that these designations are not used as pointing to actual parties formed and subsisting among the Corinthians, but (2) as representing the spirit with which they contended against one another, being the sayings of individuals, and not of parties.[6]

It is clear, therefore, that Paul has no organized denomination in mind in either Galatians or I Corinthians. Even so, it must be admitted that *haireseis* and personal contentions have always resulted in dissension and partisanship such as the ancient division between the Eastern and Western churches, and the separation between the Lutherans and Zwinglians following the dispute over the interpretation of the Lord's Supper. However, in view of fallen human nature can we not say that such fleshly conflicts are, as Paul says, necessary "in order that those who are approved may become apparent among you" (I Corinthians 11:19)? Paul is saying here that for the vindication of truth in a perverted world, dissensions are necessary.

Denominations considered as branches of the church, who work hand in hand in proclaiming the true gospel of Jesus Christ with different emphases regarding the same basic truths, should not be considered sinful as such. It is only when a sectarian spirit, denominational prejudice, is shown that it should be deplored and denounced. It seems to me that the principle of Christian liberty could be applied here again.

Stanley Lowell in his book *The Ecumenical Mirage* has demonstrated from the history of the Christian church that organizational unity is not a healthy condition for a religious faith. It has always brought about stagnation and decline, such as in the Roman Church before the

[6]*Ibid.,* II, p. 476.

Reformation and in the Anglican Church before the Wesleyan movement. Religious renewal has frequently been the result of the proliferating of movements. It is also true that religious renewal frequently results in dissension and division. Jesus' movement was a proliferating movement. Paul broke away from Judaism. Martin Luther, John Wesley, and many other religious leaders (perhaps Watchman Nee could be included here) who have brought revivals to the church, have been great proliferators.

It should also be pointed out that when the "Little Flock" refuses to recognize other denominations as churches and becomes rigidly exclusive, it is showing a sectarian spirit and is guilty of creating a new sect to do away with all sects.

The most distinctive feature of Nee's ecclesiology is, of course, his insistence on the principle of "one church at one locality." It is true that the New Testament does name the churches after the cities they were located in. And in places like Jerusalem and Ephesus where there were too many believers to be accommodated in one assembly there were several assemblies, probably meeting in houses. In Ephesus, for example, there were several centers of meeting, such as the hall of Tyrannus, the house of Aquila, and the dwelling places of other believers. When Paul refers to the Christians in these different assemblies in the same city he does not, we have seen, refer to them as "the churches," but as "the church" in that city. It is true, too, that when Paul summoned the church officials to meet him at Miletus, they were referred to as "the presbyters," not of the churches, but "of the church at Ephesus." And it is from facts like these that Nee makes his inference.

But do such Scriptural references actually teach that it is mandatory that there be only one church in one city? I think, before we can answer this question, we must first of all look into the New Testament's usage of the term "church." The primary meaning of the term is a group of believers, rather than an organization.[7] Nee himself points this out to us when he says that the first group of Christians in Jerusalem, even before there were any visible signs of organization, were called the church.[8] According to Deissmann the word "church" in the New Testament primarily means "the (convened) assembly," regarding God as the convener.[9] Louis Berkhof also regards it as primarily designating "a circle of believers in some definite locality, a local church, irrespective of the question whether these believers are or are not assembled for worship."[10] Were we to say "The whole school came to Christ," we would have the people in mind primarily and not the school as an organization. The usage for "church" is parallel. If we agree that the word was primarily used to designate a group of believers, and that the idea of organization was secondary and was added to the original meaning later, then we can begin to see Nee's theory differently, because his principle of "one church at one locality" requires that the word mean an organized church. The church in Corinth means the people of God in Corinth, and the church in Ephesus means the believers that meet in the city of Ephesus. The reference to "the church in Aquila's house" (Romans 16:5) also means the believers that meet in Aquila's house, or this would violate Nee's theory of "one church at one locality." Although there were several assemblies in

---

[7]It is enlightening to notice that Luther in his German translation of the New Testament used the word "congregation" instead of "church" and the New English Bible also uses the word "congregation" instead of "church." Thus "the church at Corinth" should read "the congregation at Corinth."

[8]See pp. 40, 41.

[9]Adolph Deissmann, *Light from the Ancient East*, trans. by L. R. M. Strachan (New York: George H. Doran Co., 1927), p. 112.

[10]Louis Berkhof, *Systematic Theology* (Grand Rapids: Wm. B. Eerdmans Publishing Co., 1968), p. 556.

Ephesus, Paul still refers to them as the "church" in Ephesus. Paul simply means the group of Christians in Ephesus. It should be pointed out, on the other hand, that I am not denying that there was an organization of the church in New Testament times. But no one can deny that the New Testament *nowhere teaches explicitly* that there should be only one organized church in one locality or city. In fact, the Bible nowhere tells us how these different assemblies in the same city were organized. So it seems to me that it is overly dogmatic to insist that there must be only one organized church in one locality.

Having pointed out what I consider can be said against Nee's approach to ecclesiology, I should like to proceed to discuss his strong points and positive contributions.

First of all we must give him credit for his sincerity and effort in upholding the Reformation principle of *Sola Scriptura* in working out a rigidly Biblical system of ecclesiology. His attempt, as we see in his *Rethinking Our Missions,* is to retrace the steps of the development of the early church starting from Antioch and to follow accordingly. In an age when the inspired written record of revelation is being dishonored in many quarters, Nee's effort is doubly significant. All the confusion and turmoil in our church today, and the unscriptural endeavor to build a single ecclesiastical monolith in the world, stem from our failure to take God's Word seriously and to conduct God's business according to His Word. Although Nee is at times overly dogmatic, yet on the whole his ecclesiology is sound. Even if it is not taken as the *only* correct pattern of church activity, it might well be acknowledged as *one of the most Biblical* patterns. It is highly practicable and has been (and still is) used by God not only in China but in many parts of Asia. Its Bible-centered nature accounts for its appeal to many sincere Christians who see that the modern churches, even conservative ones, are drifting away from the Bible in many of their practices.

Nee also sees clearly that the Protestant churches have gradually lost sight of another Reformation principle—the priesthood of all believers. He deplores the fact that the Protestant ministerial system has gradually degenerated to become like the Roman priestly mediatorial system. This, according to him, is the cause of stagnation and passivity on the part of much of the laity. Thus he emphasizes the deployment of all believers in the service of Christ. All must serve or there will be no church, declares Nee. The rapid growth of the "Little Flock" in the past few decades is due precisely to their leaders' ability to mobilize the entire church in evangelism and emigration.

One characteristic emphasis of evangelical Christianity has always been the faithful preaching of the Word to lead men to trust in Christ. But often our churches become so preoccupied with winning souls that they forget to give nurture and training to these new-born infants. Leon Morris points out this fault in his article on "current religious thought" in a recent issue of *Christianity Today*,[11] and remarks that many inside the church are beginning to look again at the doctrine of sanctification or Christian growth because of a widespread acknowledgment of the weakness of most institutional churches in this area. Nee saw the importance of training, nurture, and the deepening of the Christian's spiritual life from the beginning of his ministry in 1920. The doctrine of sanctification, showing the way to a victorious Christian life, has always occupied a foremost position in Nee's ministry. When his *Normal Christian Life* was first published in English some years ago it immediately captured the attention of

---

[11]Leon Morris, "On Being the People of God," *Christianity Today*, (December 19, 1969), p. 40.

Western Christians, who, as Leon Morris points out, are beginning to see the need for a re-emphasis of the matter of Christian growth. It has since been a very popular book, hailed as a spiritual classic. Yes, if we want to return and practice the Reformation principle of the "priesthood of all believers" we must begin by educating and training our believers so that they will become both willing and able to serve.

In his attack on denominationalism Nee points out things that should be recognized by the denominational churches. First of all, many denominations do show exclusiveness and prejudice. Refusal to recognize one another and to cooperate does weaken the witness of the gospel and make Christendom look schismatic and ugly. It is true too, as Nee points out, that the larger denominations very often tend to rely on their well-ordered organizational machinery rather than on God, resulting in lifelessness and stagnation. Nee's movement in China did awaken the denominational churches from their slothful complacency and their dependence on foreign financial support.

I must say, from personal observation, that Chinese Christians in general do not have very strong denominational feelings. It is hoped that Western missionaries among the Chinese will help to foster instead of weaken this healthy tendency to minimize and de-emphasize denominational differences. The feeling an ordinary Chinese believer has about belonging to a Presbyterian Church rather than an Anglican Church, for instance, is no stronger than your feeling about shopping at the A&P or Jewels. There is much interdenominational activity. Speakers from other denominations are often invited to speak and conduct services. My experience with various denominational churches in North America in recent years has all the more convinced me that if there is anything the churches of the West can learn from the younger churches of the Orient, it is this readiness to accept each other as fellow Christians.

Some Comments on Lee's Ideas

The Kingdom

In Chapter Three we devoted a considerable amount of space to the discussion of Witness Lee's view of the Kingdom of God and the Kingdom of heaven. You will recall that he makes a clear-cut distinction between the Kingdom of God and the Kingdom of heaven. He also regards the entering of the Kingdom of heaven to be a reward for those prepared or watchful Christians called "the overcomers." In other words, only those who overcome can enter the Kingdom of heaven in the millennium; the other Christians will be punished during the millennium and then allowed to join the overcomers in the New Jerusalem. Such dogmatic pronouncements in the difficult field of Biblical eschatology deserve some comment. It is this view of the Kingdom, together with other daring statements—such as his challenge to all orthodox Christians that the Bible nowhere teaches that the washing of Jesus' blood alone gets us to heaven (in Chinese, it is paradise)—that has caused many to label Lee as a heretic. A symposium prepared by a group of Chinese writers, intended to refute such erratic views of Lee's, was published some years ago under the editorship of Chan Pui Yan.

A distinction between the Kingdom of God and the Kingdom of heaven is frequently considered by many non-dispensationalists, such as G. E. Ladd, to be the essential basis of dispensationalism, especially the "postponed kingdom" theory.[12] However, leading dispensationalists

---

[12]George E. Ladd, *Crucial Questions About the Kingdom of God* (Grand Rapids: Wm. B. Eerdmans Publishing Co., 1952), pp. 101–117.

like John F. Walvoord and Charles C. Ryrie of Dallas Theological Seminary *deny* that their position is based on a distinction between the Kingdom of God and the Kingdom of heaven.[13] Within dispensational circles there are many who do not make any such distinction. A. J. McClain of Grace Theological Seminary in his *The Greatness of the Kingdom,* and Erich Sauer of Germany in his *The Triumph of the Crucified,* for instance, maintain no such distinction. This should be pointed out at the outset, lest any friends of dispensationalism wrongly think that I am attacking their system when I show that Witness Lee's view of the Kingdom is untenable.

Biblical scholars of both the liberal and conservative persuasions have long recognized the importance of the Kingdom concept in the teaching of our Lord. But the intense research and scrutiny devoted to the subject by many able students of the Word has not enabled them to arrive at a generally accepted opinion on the subject; instead there has arisen a host of radically different interpretations. (G. E. Ladd, in his book *Crucial Questions About the Kingdom of God,* gives a very good survey of the history of interpretation on the matter.) However, it *is* generally agreed that the word "kingdom" is not an exact translation of the Hebrew *malkuth* and the Aramaic equivalent *malkutha,* or of the Greek *basileia,* and that the Biblical data do not support the view that holds to a distinction between the two designations, the Kingdom of God and the Kingdom of heaven.[14]

The English word "kingdom" is always associated with the idea of a territory to be governed. But philologists point out to us that the Greek word *basileia,* with a few exceptions, should actually be translated "sovereign

[13]Charles C. Ryrie, *Dispensationalism Today* (Chicago: Moody Press, 1965), pp. 170, 171.

[14]A. M. Hunter, *The Work and Words of Jesus* (Philadelphia: The Westminster Press, 1950), p. 69.

rule" or "kingly reign."

What concerns us here is the second point of agreement among modern scholars: that there is no difference of meaning between "the kingdom of God" and the "kingdom of heaven." A look at Young's *Concordance of the Holy Bible* reveals that the last three Gospels, Mark, Luke, and John, use the expression "the kingdom of God" quite consistently. Matthew, on the other hand, uses "the kingdom of heaven" except in five places: 6:33; 12:28; 19:24; 21:31; and 21:43.

Why then does Matthew use the term "the kingdom of heaven?" The answer to the question is found in the fact that Matthew was writing to the Jews, who were well known for their avoidance of the ineffable name. Another name was usually employed to designate God. Thus the word "heaven" was used instead of the word "God" in the expression "the kingdom of heaven." But when the other Evangelists wrote with the Gentiles in mind, they realized that the designation "the kingdom of heaven" would mean nothing to them. The Gentiles would wonder what "kingdom of the skies" or "kingdom of the blue" meant. That is why these writers used "the kingdom of God" throughout their Gospels.

The similarites of the first three Gospels (commonly called the Synoptic Gospels) lead many to believe that the three writers were dependent on one another, one way or another, in writing their Gospels. The most common explanation is that Mark, the simplest and shortest account, was the first Gospel, and the other two Synoptics were based on Mark's account with the addition of other materials. Whatever the explanation of the Synoptic phenomena might be, one thing is clear: They all record many sayings and doings of our Lord in similar fashion. This enables us to assume that whenever two or sometimes three of them report on the same event or saying of the Lord, the variation in the use of words is merely a language matter. Thus when reporting the same saying of Jesus, if Matthew uses "the kingdom of heaven" and the others use "the kingdom of God"—and especially if this occurs quite frequently—we can be sure that they are interchangeable terms which mean exactly the same thing.

In Matthew 4:17 it is recorded that after John the Baptist was imprisoned, Jesus came out to declare that the "kingdom of heaven" was at hand. But in Mark 1:14,15 the same event is reported and "the kingdom of God" is used. Again, all three of the Synoptics contain the same Kingdom parables. In Matthew the expression "the kingdom of heaven" is used (Chapter 13); but in Mark (Chapter 4) and Luke (Chapter 8) "the kingdom of God" is used instead. We also see that all three Synoptics record Jesus' famous saying when He called the little children to come to Him. In Matthew 19:14 we read: "But Jesus said, Suffer little children, and forbid them not, to come unto me: for of such is the kingdom of heaven." In Mark 10:14 we have ". . . Suffer the little children to come unto me, and forbid them not: for of such is the kingdom of God." In Luke 18:16 it is: ". . . Suffer little children to come unto me, and forbid them not: for of such is the kingdom of God." We notice that Matthew uses "the kingdom of heaven," while Mark and Luke use "the kingdom of God."

There are other such examples in the Synoptics where the Evangelists use "the kingdom of heaven" in one place and "the kingdom of God" in another to report the same sayings of our Lord. There is no other explanation to this than the fact that they are interchangeable expressions which mean exactly the same thing.[15] If there were indeed some crucial difference in the two designations, our Lord

[15]Some do explain the interchangeability by pointing out that "the kingdom of God" is an inclusive term. However, this still cannot account for Jesus' failure to explain the differences.

failed to explain it to the disciples. Could it be that the Evangelists and other Christians for nearly two thousand years have failed to discern such a decisive theological difference in terminology?

That both Jesus and Matthew use "the kingdom of heaven" and "the kingdom of God" undiscriminatingly to indicate the exact same thing is best shown in the story of the rich young man recorded in Matthew 19. After the young man went away sorrowfully, a conversation between Jesus and His disciples was carried on as follows:

> Then said Jesus unto his disciples, Verily I say unto you, That a rich man shall hardly enter into the *kingdom of heaven*. And again I say unto you, It is easier for a camel to go through the eye of a needle, than for a rich man to enter into the *kingdom of God*. When his disciples heard it, they were exceedingly amazed, saying, Who then can be *saved?* (Matthew 19:23–25).

Let us observe here that Jesus uses both "the kingdom of heaven" and "the kingdom of God" in the same breath. The disciples have no problem knowing what Jesus means, and equate the two expressions with salvation. The inevitable conclusion again is that Jesus considers the two expressions as meaning the same thing and that He uses them interchangeably in His conversation. In passing, it should be pointed out that Luke has the same account, and Jesus is there reported as using "the kingdom of God" twice (Luke 18:24–26). Mark, too, records the same conversation (10:23–26), and there Jesus uses "the kingdom of God" three times.

Those who try to read into the phrases something that is not there, as Lee has done, always have to resort to the dangerous practice of wresting Scripture (II Peter 3:16). This Lee does when he cites I Corinthians 5:1–5 and 6:9,10 to prove that the Bible teaches that to enter the Kingdom of heaven is different from possessing eternal life. According to him, one may be born again and yet not be able to enter the Kingdom of heaven in the millennium (see p. 59). In I Corinthians 5:5, the man who committed fornication was delivered "unto Satan for the destruction of the flesh, that the spirit may be saved in the day of the Lord Jesus." Later, in 6:9,10, Paul says: "Know ye not that the unrighteous shall not inherit the kingdom of God? Be not deceived: neither fornicators, nor idolaters, nor adulterers, nor effeminate, nor abusers of themselves with mankind, nor thieves, nor covetous, nor drunkards, nor revilers, nor extortioners, shall inherit the kingdom of God." To Lee's great disappointment Paul uses "the kingdom of God" here. In order to make the Bible fit his own system Lee has to twist the Scripture by insisting that "to inherit the Kingdom of God" means the same as "to enter the Kingdom of heaven." Actually, in I Corinthians 5 Paul is simply saying that the fornicator should be expelled from the church, hoping that he might be led to repentance after God allows Satan to inflict sufferings on his flesh. In Chapter 6, Paul warns the fornicators and others that if they continue to live immoral lives, it shows that they are not truly born-again Christians—and, hence, that they will not enter the Kingdom of God. We have also just pointed out that for Jesus "the kingdom of heaven," "the kingdom of God," and "salvation" all mean the same thing. In other words, to be saved is to enter the Kingdom of heaven. In the face of such strong and clear Biblical evidence, it is the words of Jesus against the words of Witness Lee. Lee has to choose between our Lord and his own system; he has to choose his own way of salvation or our Lord's way of salvation.

Another strong emphasis of Lee and his followers in recent years has been the division of believers into two classes, the "overcomers" who will be raptured before the tribulation and enjoy the reign with Christ in the Kingdom of heaven during the millennium, and the "unprepared believers" who will be punished before joining the overcomers in the New Jerusalem.

The word "overcome" or "conquer" appears twenty-two times in the New Testament. The Apostle John uses it once in his Gospel, six times in his First Epistle, and eleven times in the book of Revelation. Thus the word is used almost exclusively by John. The questions we have to ask are: What do they overcome? How do they overcome? And finally, who are the overcomers?

In the seven letters of Revelation the verb "overcome" is absolute, without any object expressed. However, in I John the objects to be overcome are "the world" and our adversary, Satan (I John 2:13,14; 4:4; 5:4,5; also John 16:33 and Rev. 12:11). The word "world " here stands for the totality of all the influences and forces in the human world that are hostile to God. Since Satan is regarded as the Prince of this "world," it is clear that John is referring to the overcoming of Satan and all the anti-God forces of this world led by Satan.

How do we overcome? John in his First Epistle tells us: "For whatsoever is born of God overcometh the world: and this is the victory that overcometh the world, even our faith. Who is he that overcometh the world, but he that believeth that Jesus is the Son of God?" (I John 5:4,5). Again in Revelation 12:11 he says, "And they overcame him by the blood of the Lamb, and by the word of their testimony; and they loved not their lives unto the death." It is clear from these statements that the overcomers overcome by faith in the redemptive work of Christ on the cross, which leads to regeneration, and by their testimony and good works as outward evidence of their genuine faith. The overcomers overcome because Christ has overcome for them (John 16:33). They show this victory by their good works or testimony, as in the case of the martyrs in Revelation 12, whose willingness to suffer shows that they are true believers.

This leads us to the last question: Who are the overcomers? The declaration of I John 5:4,5 indicates that they are simply born-again Christians, those who genuinely believe that Jesus is the Son of God. In other words, the overcomers are all truly born-again believers.

All this leads to the conclusion that "to overcome" is the equivalent of "to be saved" in Pauline terminology; "overcomer" is another word for "believer." John is simply speaking of the believer's true status in Christ rather than what he has gained, namely salvation. From God's point of view, the issue is justification by grace through faith; and from the human point of view, in Johannine terminology, it is overcoming by faith in the blood of Jesus.

Thus John is only speaking about the distinction between the regenerated and the unregenerated, believers and mere professors. It is Biblically unwarranted to divide regenerated believers into "prepared" and "unprepared" believers, "overcomers" and "those who fail to overcome." All the scriptures cited by Lee to prove that there is such a distinction between "prepared" and "unprepared" believers should be explained in the light of the difference between the regenerated and the unregenerated.

Lee's doctrine of a partial rapture also has no Biblical support at all. It is not within the scope of our study to discuss the rapture question at this juncture. It is enough to point out here that within conservative circles the partial rapture position is no longer an option. Those who are interested in a refutation of this theory should read J. D. Pentecost's *Things to Come* (pp. 156–161).

Lee's special doctrine of "entering the Kingdom of heaven" stands or falls on whether or not his distinction made between the "the Kingdom of God" and "the Kingdom of heaven" and his classification of regenerated believers into "those who overcome" and "those who do not overcome" can be substantiated by the Word of God. We have already demonstrated that this distinction and classification cannot be made without twisting Scripture. Our Lord and His apostles equate entering the Kingdom of heaven with salvation. Once again we must ask Lee to make a choice between the clear teaching of Scripture and his own system.

Baptism

Lee's view of baptism also deserves some comment. We have already pointed out in Chapter Four that his view of baptism is similar to that of the Roman Catholic Church which believes it to be a rite actually conferring grace and producing holiness—though he, of course, does not teach *infant* baptism. You may recall that Lee defines baptism as a practical procedure and an actual step through which we unite with Christ and receive salvation. Such sacramental understanding of baptism, *i.e.*, baptismal regeneration, is unbiblical and should be rejected.

Lee's erroneous view stems from a misunderstanding both of certain Scriptural references and of the doctrine of salvation. He cites John 3:5 which says that "Except a man be born of water and of the Spirit, he cannot enter into the kingdom of God" and concludes that the "water" here refers to baptism. It should be pointed out at once that Jesus does not say "water baptism" but merely "water." It is wrong to jump to a conclusion and decide that the "water" must necessarily refer to baptism.

The context of this verse is very important in understanding what "water" means. We remember that in this chapter Nicodemus, a Pharisee and a ruler of the Jews, came to see Jesus and was immediately told that he must be born again of water and the Spirit. We must bear in mind that the Jews believed that as descendants of Abraham and as the Covenant people of God they were automatically saved, and that they pleased God by observing both the moral laws and certain religious ceremonials such as ritual washings and circumcision. Jesus told them time and again that sacrifices and the observance of the laws and rites could not save them. In other words, they must not equate the Kingdom of God with physical ceremonials (Mark 7:1–23; Rom. 3:24 ff; Gal. 5:2–6). When Jesus saw Nicodemus He knew, of course, that he was a typical Jew with a typical Jewish understanding of salvation. So our Lord immediately pointed out to him that he must be born again if he wanted to enter the Kingdom of God. It is thus quite inconceivable that our Lord would appoint baptism, *another ceremonial,* as a condition for salvation. Salvation is regarded throughout the entire New Testament as by grace and through faith alone. Thus to interpret "water" in John 3:5 as referring to water baptism can only be ignorance of the clear New Testament teaching on salvation. To say that baptism is necessary for salvation is to turn salvation by grace into salvation by works, an abomination for Paul.

The concepts of "water" and "spirit" go back to Ezekiel 36:25–27, where "water" signifies cleansing from sin and impurities and "spirit" signifies inner renovation. It is clear, therefore, that in John 3:5 our Lord is using "water" and "the spirit" to describe both the negative and positive sides of regeneration, the removal of sin and the new birth by the Spirit.

Lee also quotes scriptures to show that baptism is always connected with faith and salvation (Acts 22:16 and Mark 16:16). However, it should be recognized that when baptism and salvation are put together, the one is not necessarily the condition for obtaining the other. Baptism is important not as a condition for salvation but as a testimony and sign of salvation before men. Baptism symbolizes our regeneration through union with Christ in His death, burial, and resurrection (Rom. 6:1 ff). It is thus a tes-

timony—and a willingness to testify is a sign of one's
regeneration. In the same way, works is not necessary
for obtaining salvation. But salvation necessarily produces
good works, and the lack of good works or the fruit
of the Spirit before the eyes of men shows that a person
is not regenerate. It is in this light that we understand
James' statements that works are necessary for salvation.
And it is the same light that enables us to understand
the close connection between baptism and salvation in the
Bible. For Jesus says, "Whosoever therefore shall confess
me before men, him will I confess also before my Father
which is in heaven" (Matt. 10:32). If a believer refuses
to confess Christ by baptism before men, he is not a
true believer. It is in this sense that baptism is so important
for salvation. It also explains Jesus' words in the Great
Commission that "He that believeth and is baptized shall
be saved" (Mark 16:16). It is true that in the Great Commission the commands are to preach the gospel, to teach,
and to baptize. But the emphasis is on making disciples
by preaching the gospel, and not on baptism. Paul did
not personally baptize his converts except one or two.
He says emphatically, "I thank God that I baptized none
of you, but Crispus and Gaius; lest any should say that
I had baptized in mine own name. And I baptized also
the household of Stephanas: besides, I know not whether
I baptized any other. For Christ sent me not to baptize,
but to preach the gospel: not with wisdom of words,
lest the cross of Christ should be made of none effect"
(I Cor. 1:14–17). If baptism is necessary for salvation,
as Lee imagines, how dare Paul say: "For Christ sent me
not to baptize, but to preach the gospel."

Lee also cites I Peter 3:21 to show that "baptism doth
also now save us." A careful reader of Scripture would
discover that Peter in the immediate context is speaking
figuratively. As the "water" of the flood saved Noah,
so also water baptism symbolizes (in KJV terminology

"the like figure") our salvation. The Chinese version also says explicitly in verse 21 that it is the baptism that is pictured or signified by this water (the water of Noah's flood). It is the spiritual reality symbolized by the water of baptism that saves. The sentence construction here is very difficult and involved in the Greek language. A quotation from K. N. Taylor's *Living New Testament* will help us to understand the meaning of this verse:

> That, by the way, is what baptism pictures for us: in baptism we show that we have been saved from death and doom by the resurrection of Christ; not because our bodies are washed clean by the water, but because in being baptized we are turning to God and asking Him to cleanse our *hearts* from sin.

The meaning of this verse should also be understood in light of the New Testament's total teaching on the relationship between baptism and salvation that we have just discussed. We are not saved by baptism, but by the regenerating power of God and the redemptive work of Christ symbolized by the rite of water baptism. This is substantially what Peter is speaking about here.

Lee's erroneous view of the meaning of baptism and its efficacy to remove our sin has led him in recent years to the practice of baptizing individuals again and again (see the Appendix). His doctrine calls for such a practice because this is the natural result of his basic interpretation regarding baptism.

Allegorizing

In addition to the wresting of Scripture to fit his own scheme of things, unintentional though this may be, another mistake of Lee's—a mistake which moves one ever further from an orthodox position and can eventually lead into heresy—is his extreme fondness for a typical and allegorical approach in his understanding of God's

Word. All modern evangelical students of Scripture would agree that the only totally sound method of interpretation is the historical-grammatical method. Most conservative scholars appeal for extreme caution and limited use of the typical method, while almost all faithful students of the Word reject the allegorical approach. The renowned scholar Bernard Ramm sums up the faults and dangers of allegorizing Scripture in these words:

> The curse of the allegorical method is that it obscures the true meaning of the Word of God and had it not kept the Gospel truth central it would have become cultic and heretical. In fact, this is exactly what happened when the Gnostics allegorized the New Testament. The Bible treated allegorically becomes putty in the hands of the exegete. Different doctrinal systems could emerge within the framework of allegorical hermeneutics and no way would exist to determine which were the true. . . . The allegorical method puts a premium on the subjective and the doleful result is the obstruction of the Word of God.[16]

The above quotation must come as a shock to those who accept Lee's teachings because it describes exactly what is happening through Lee's misuse of the Holy Word. When one interprets Scripture with the understanding that "In today's universe all the material symbolizes the spiritual,"[17] one always comes to the Scripture with the idea that there is some other meaning beneath the obvious and literal statements of the Bible. Thus Lee's task in searching Scripture is to find the hidden meaning. We have already discussed at length Lee's allegorical interpretation in the area of ecclesiology, showing how he goes beyond Nee in this regard.[18]

In judging the validity of such interpretation one simply

---

[16]Bernard Ramm, *Protestant Biblical Interpretation* (Boston: W. H. Wilde Co., 1956), pp. 30, 31.

[17]See p. 37.

[18]See pp. 36–40 and pp. 48–50.

has to ask the question: What is the passage intended to teach? When Moses recorded how God put Adam to sleep, and then created Eve with Adam's rib, was the passage written to teach the formation of the church and its relationship with Christ? Are those women cited by Lee recorded to show some aspects of the church? If so, how can we know? Those fond of the allegorical method would immediately point to the illuminating work of the Holy Spirit as the answer. The problem is that all claim the illumination of the Holy Spirit—but come up with radically different interpretations of the same passage in many instances.

We remember that Lee interprets the gold and precious stones laid bare by the action of the rivers of Genesis 2 (God's life) as representing God's nature in us and our transformed personality.[19] Let us imagine that one of Lee's friends with equally good imagination comes along and challenges Lee by insisting that the rivers symbolize not God's life but God's nature in us and our transformed personality, and that the precious stones represent the fruits and good works of our transformed life. The problem is: Who is right, Lee or his friend? This is exactly where the problem and danger of the allegorical method lies. In allegorizing, the authority of our faith and practice shifts from the objective revealed Word of God to the subjective imagination of the human mind. Our religion becomes humanistic and not the religion of the Book.

It is a fact that occasionally an inspired Biblical writer has seen a hidden symbolic meaning within a simple narrative recorded by an earlier Biblical writer—such as Paul does in Galatians 4 with reference to Genesis 21, and as the author of Hebrews does in several places in his Epistle. Yet it must be realized that what Paul, writing

[19]See pp. 37,38.

Scripture under the inspiration of the Holy Spirit, could do, we cannot do. The reformers were right in insisting on interpreting scripture with scripture according to its plain historical-grammatical meaning. This implies that only the Scripture itself can grant us the right to give a certain Scriptural passage any meaning other than its plain meaning.

Thus the recent reports of Lee's unorthodox teachings come to us as no surprise. He has fallen into what Nee calls the substitution of the ministering of the dead letter of the Word for the ministering of life and spirit.[20]

Nee and Lee

Those familiar with the writings of both Nee and Lee would agree that they reflect two men of very different natural and spiritual caliber. It is a great misfortune on Lee's part that he has had to succeed Nee, a man far superior to most men both intellectually and spiritually. All outsiders who are familiar with the "Little Flock" movement admire and praise Nee highly as a great preacher, an original thinker and a spiritual giant, although they may not be in agreement with some of his views on church matters. It is a pity that Lee's extremism and unorthodox practices have caused some to reject *in toto* Nee's writings and other ministries. During the early days of the Plymouth Brethren movement there were thousands of preachers in the established churches, including such men as C. H. Spurgeon and A. J. Gordon, who had not the least sympathy for the Brethren view of the church—yet who admitted their indebtedness to them for a fuller and richer understanding of the Word. Likewise, we may reject Lee's deviations and the "peculiar church view" of the "Little Flock," yet Nee's contribution to our richer understanding of the Scripture must be retained.

[20]See p. 40.

EPILOGUE

Just before this book went to press, a reliable report reached us that Watchman Nee went to be with our Lord on June 1, 1972, after about seventy glorious years of earthly pilgrimage. His twenty-year sentence had ended some three months earlier, and he had been released from prison. It is believed that he spent his years of imprisonment doing translation work for the government. His wife had died earlier, on October 7, 1971.

This book has been written with the highest respect for this faithful and devoted servant of our Lord, hoping that it may help to preserve the spiritual insights he received.

It is our prayer that our Lord will continue to use the written words of Nee to speak to His people of our day.

Both Nee himself and the "church" he founded are not perfect. I believe that Nee would be the first to admit this. Therefore, let me emphasize once again that it would be unfair for "Little Flock" critics to attempt to do away with all the contributions to the interpretation of Bible truth made by Nee and his followers because of some of their untraditional ideas. A more profitable course of action would be to sort out the undesirable elements and retain the sound teachings. It is hoped that this little volume will serve this purpose in the area of ecclesiology.

Let me also say that it is not my purpose in writing this book to denounce the "Little Flock" and to defend denominationalism. No human effort to expound Biblical truth can claim infallibility. It is important, therefore, that we be open-minded and seek together humbly and prayerfully to understand the truth. I only hope and pray that our Lord will restore the "Little Flock" to doctrinal purity and spiritual vitality.

Someone has remarked that Chinese Christians are the products of three men: John Sung, Wang Ming Tao, and Watchman Nee. Sung was an evangelist, and since he left us with few significant writings his influence is generally not felt today. Wang Ming Tao, like Nee, is in the hands of the Communists in mainland China. His rich spoken ministry has influenced many lives. However he has no church of his own, and his writings are few; his influence is also on the decline. Watchman Nee has left behind a strong group of followers who are faithfully and enthusiastically perpetuating his teachings. His literature ministry, moreover, has preserved a large number of his sermons, devotional books, and theological works. Through these printed pages Nee's impact will continue to be felt among the Chinese and also in the West.